Cigars of the World

This edition published by
WELLFLEET PRESS
a division of Book Sales Inc.
114 Northfield Avenue
Edison, New Jersey 08837

This edition © 1997
© 1997 Copyright S.A.
55-57, rue Brillat-Savarin F-75013 PARIS-FRANCE

ISBN 0-7858-0822-1

Printed in Spain

Edited by Aurelio Pastor
with the assistance of Anne-Marie Chéné
La Casa Del Habano, Montreal
Research Alain Eid

Cigars of the World

Photographs by Fanny Bruno

THE WELLFLEET PRESS

contents

The pleasure that comes from smoking a fine cigar is an experience not to be missed, as cigar lovers will affirm. It is our hope that such a pleasure can be shared with readers through the medium of this book. Come with us on a journey through the known and unknown reaches of the world of the cigar. Our voyage spans three continents, with a look at nine various countries—a nearly complete tour of the dominions of the cigar.

The journey may not be an easy one, but it is well worth the effort in the long run. Indeed, over thirty-eight brands and many more different cigar models are presented here. The brands featured were carefully selected to meet the most demanding of criteria. One such criterion is the utmost respect for the centuries-old tradition of the Havana. Our selection reflects that tradition. The non-Havana brands featured here owe their excellence in part to the Cuban tradition which was passed down to them. In fact, the tradition's influence has been so overwhelming that it is now quasi-universal—regardless of politics, oceans and other barriers. The interest in featuring other flavors and aromas from other lands is to make the journey more varied and interesting.

We begin—naturally—in the port of Havana, with a sampling of the best Havanas currently available, such as the Esplendidos of Cohiba, the Double Corona of Punch, the Tainos of La Gloria Cubana, and the legendary Montecristo No. 2—the crown jewel of the figurados. But the terrain is rapidly changing. Davidoff has left Cuba for Santo Domingo in the Dominican Republic. Likewise, Honduras, Nicaragua, Jamaica and Mexico are no longer the backwaters of the cigar world; each in turn has become a serious rival to pre-eminent Cuba. Beyond the Caribbean, the Canary Islands and—on the other side of the world—the Philippines and Sumatra complete the journey. These are islands, or countries flanked by water. Indeed, it is as if it were through the element of water that nature found full expression of its most fragrant aromas and most refined flavors.

A tour of the various formats, flavors and qualities of the cigars making up our selection will also prove a useful introduction to the uninitiated. We consider this selection to have a broad spectrum which appeals to a variety of tastes, ranging from the robustos, ever-growing in popularity, to the more modest formats that are ideal for beginners. We also highlight the more imposing, luxurious formats, with particular attention given to several double coronas and a number of churchills, a format that is often a hallmark of many of the best brands.

Cuba

Fonseca, Cohiba, Romeo y Julieta, Rafael Gonzales, Partagas, Punch, Montecristo, El Rey del Mundo, Ramon Allones... A few of the most celebrated brands in the five hundred years of cigar history.

When Christopher Columbus arrived in 1492, Cuba was populated by the Tainos Indians, who had been smoking tobacco for centuries.

Cubans are renowned throughout the world for the manufacturing of fine cigars. A long tradition of excellence lies behind their craftsmanship, which involves the same attention to detail devoted to the production of fine wines or the manufacturing of the best perfumes.

This tradition dates back centuries and is largely responsible for the unchallenged quality of this most famous of Cuban products. Indeed, such names as Cohiba, Montecristo, Hoyo de Monterrey and El Rey del Mundo are familiar to connoisseurs everywhere. This tradition is founded on the best tobacco-growing land in the world, the best plants and naturally the best leaves, without mentioning further the well-known skills of the manufacturers themselves. Every one of these magnificent *puros* is the creation of no fewer than one hundred and seventy successive operations, each one the work of an artisan, beginning with the tobacco grower and ending with the master sampler.

The history of this tradition begins well before the arrival of Christopher Columbus in 1492 and dates back to the first inhabitants of the island, the Tainos Indians. In fact, the word "tobacco" is the Tainos word for cigar, what they called the long, leaf cylinders they used for rolling and smoking the dried tobacco leaves. The word was appropriated by the newcomers and came to signify the tobacco plant itself, although to this day in Cuba the word is still used in its original meaning. Nevertheless, the Indian "tobacco" was only a primitive prototype of what eventually became the cigar. The *puro,* as it is commonly called, was invented by the Spanish during the seventeenth century. The key feature of this invention consisted of the double packaging of the tobacco in its recognizable form. Cloaked in a wrapper leaf, the cigar is made of an intermediate binder which contains the filler, or the tobacco itself. Perhaps the most important innovation of the Spanish was the introduction of a more aromatic species of plant which they had discovered in Mexico. This superior leaf, *Nicotiana tabacum,* replaced the indigenous species and is the ancestor of ninety percent of the different tobacco varieties currently consumed throughout the world.

For centuries, the tobacco industry was monopolized by Seville, which depended on the cultivation of *Nicotiana tabacum* in Cuba. Cuban planters were therefore obliged to restrict themselves to the local production of cigars, which they peddled to sailors passing through Havana. Despite the monopoly by Seville, these local products became known as the best throughout the world. Not until 1821 did a local tobacco industry come into being, when Spain finally accorded Cubans the right to export their own products.

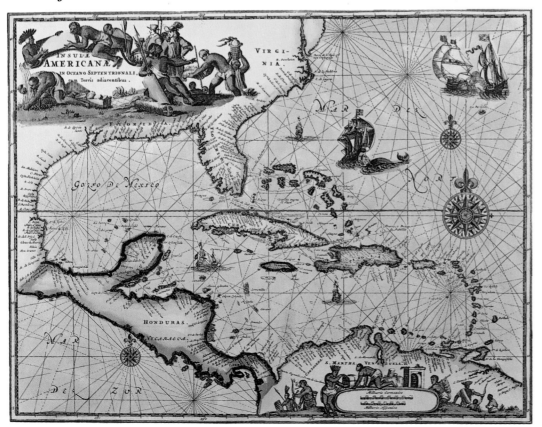

Two-thirds of the total production is of a rather mediocre quality, made from the strongest tobacco grown on the island, commonly in the regions of Remedios and Oriente. These cigars are smoked by the Cubans themselves. The other third are reserved for export and are made of the highest quality tobacco. These cigars are, of course, the famous Havanas. The best tobacco-growing lands are reserved for the cultivation of the export varieties, mostly situated in the area known as Partido in the province of Havana and more famously in the area known as the Vuelta Abajo in the very west of the island— "the land of the best tobacco in the world," as it is said in Cuba. The climate and the soil in these areas are ideal for the cultivation of tobacco. The top soil is deep, mineral rich and sandy, and temperatures average 78°F with about sixty-five percent humidity yearly. The tobacco-growing lands are divided into *vegas,* which are the tobacco-grower's equivalent of vineyards. Best known to cigar lovers are the *vegas* of San Juan and San Luis y Martinez, which are reputed to furnish the finest tobacco wrappers. The tobacco planters themselves are known as *vegueros,* and there are approximately fifteen thousand of them on the island. For the most part, these are small, private growers whose farms, or *fincas,* are rarely larger than a few acres.

Two varieties of plants are used in the manufacturing of a Havana: the *corojo,* which provides the leaf for the wrapper, and the *criollo de sol,* which provides the binder and the filler. Growing the *corojo* requires the most care. It is cultivated under expansive cotton tarpaulins, the *tapados,* which protect the plants from intense sunlight and against strong winds and parasites. Each plant yields sixteen to seventeen leaves which, in the end, are used to make thirty or so wrappers. The *criollo de sol* grow in the open air and have only twelve to fourteen leaves per plant.

The leaves acquire different aromatic qualities depending on the length of time they are exposed to the sun, and this is what results in the different varieties of tobacco. Three different varieties are used for the filler: the *ligero,* the *seco* and the *volado.* The *ligero* comes from the uppermost leaves of the plant and yields the most flavorful tobacco. The *seco,* which comes from the leaves of the middle part of the plant, is a lighter variety of tobacco that has a more subtle aroma. The *volado,* lastly, comes from the lower part of the plant. It is

The result was the *furia cubana,* or the sudden proliferation of hundreds of different brands, with more than two hundred existing by 1848. A number of them are still around today. Among the "historic" brands still being enjoyed are: Por Larrañaga (1834), Ramon Allones (1837), Punch (1840), H. Upmann (1844), Partagas (1845) El Rey del Mundo (1848), Romeo y Julieta (1850) and Hoyo de Monterrey (1867).

Over three hundred and fifty million cigars are manufactured in Cuba each year. A true Havana, however, is not just any cigar produced in Havana.

The torcedores (top), who roll the cigars, make up an elite work force that commands a lot of respect in Cuba. Their skills are such that the amount of tobacco rolled never varies by more than an infinitesimal amount from one cigar to the next. Each torcedor (which literally means "twister") has the right to smoke as many cigars as he or she wants, provided they are smoked at work (above). The image of Che Guevara, head of cigar production in Cuba in the early 1960's, is still present in the factories seen here (far right).

A tobacco plantation in the Vuelta Abajo, one of the principal tobacco-growing regions, situated in the west of the island. The region's red soil is reputed to be the best tobacco-growing soil in the world. It is a long, laborious process: from the planting of seeds in September until the harvest in February, each plant is inspected at least one hundred and fifty times by the vegueros, the tobacco growers.

Following the harvest, the leaves are stored in special warehouses, the casas de tabaco, where they are air dried (air curing). The leaves are sewn together in pairs and hung over wooden hangars. As the leaves are cured, the chlorophyll disappears and the leaves assume the familiar golden brown color of tobacco.

Before the banding and the packaging, the escogedor, *or color expert, separates the cigars according to their different tints (above). His job is to assure that the cigars in each box all have the same color (below). The* escogedor *is capable of distinguishing with the naked eye the sixty-five different shades of brown that a Cuban wrapper can have. Today this job has been made a lot easier: in the past, the* escogedor *was required to differentiate between two hundred variants of brown. Among the most common colors figure the* clarissimo *(green), the* claro claro *(light), the* claro *(beige), the* colorado *(reddish brown), the* colorado claro *(light brown), the* maduro colorado *(dark brown), the* maduro *(brown-black) and the* oscuro *or* negro *(black).*

the least flavorful of the varieties and its principal role is to assure that the cigar burns properly. Each plant, from the time it is planted until the time insecticides are applied, is inspected about one hundred and fifty times by the *vegueros,* and harvesting is done by hand. Each variety of leaf is picked at different times of the season depending upon its degree of maturity. An average of forty days elapses, for example, before the *corojo* has been completely harvested.

Once the harvest is finished, the *vegueros* then begin preparation of the tobacco. The leaves are stocked in *casas de tabacos* where they are hung out to dry. This process of "air curing" can last up to two months during which the chlorophyll in the leaves disappears and the tobacco assumes its familiar golden brown color. At this point, only the acidity in the leaves remains to be removed. This acidity exists in the form of a resin that is still quite prevalent in the leaves and renders the tobacco completely unfit for consumption. Two successive fermentations are necessary to expel the resin from the leaf. For the export variety, a third fermentation is employed. This fermentation is done by the manufacturers and can last from one to three years depending upon the quality of the tobacco. Some wrappers are even fermented as long as ten years. The work ends at the plantation with the *escogida,* the big "selection festival" when the

State buyers arrive to choose the leaves that will be sent to the manufacturers. A new cycle in the production of a Havana begins—that of actually manufacturing the cigar itself.

In the past, each brand of cigar had its own *fabrica,* or manufacturer. There were as many as one thousand three hundred in the last century, traditionally clustered around Havana. The 1959 revolution has somewhat simplified the situation. Today, six principal manufacturers share the most famous brands, those reserved for exportation. They are known as Francisco Perez German, Briones Montoto, José Martí, Fernando Roig, Carlos Balino and El Laguito. This last manufacturer, opened in 1960, serves as a model for the others. Its workshops produce Cohiba, Trinidad and a few types of Montecristo at a volume of ten thousand cigars each day. The manufacturer Briones Montoto produces as many as thirty-two thousand cigars a day, including Romeo y Julieta, Sancho Panza and Rafael Gonzales. A similar volume is produced by the manufacturer Francisco Perez German, which furnishes six well-known brands: Partagas, Ramon Allones, Bolivar, La Gloria Cubana, a few of the Cohiba and a few of the Montecristo.

The *tabaqueros* are the manufacturer's skilled laborers. They make up a long chain of different functions by which the cigar ultimately takes its

form. The master-mixer is the first link in the chain. It is his job to gather together all of the leaves that will be used for the exterior wrappers. This is a crucial role to play since he is ultimately responsible for guaranteeing the unvarying quality of the leaves from year to year, as well as the brand of cigar which they are used to manufacture. The selected tobacco and leaves finally reach the *galera* (the gallery), where perhaps the most delicate operation takes place. This is where the *torcedores*, or cigar rollers, practice their art. There are over three hundred *torcedores* at Briones Montoto, occupying small workshops side by side. Their only tool is an oval-shaped blade, the *chaveta*. It takes a *torcedor* five minutes to roll a cigar. The filling is shaped in the palm of the hand, rolled in the inner wrapper and finally in the outer wrapper. Of course, it is easier said than done. It takes six years of practice to learn how to properly roll a Havana by hand. A tried and true "roller" can roll as many as one hundred and twenty cigars each day. His or her skill is such that the difference in weight from one cigar never varies by more than an infinitesimal amount regardless of the kind of cigar being rolled.

Once it exits the *galera*, the cigar will be stored for one month in a special conditioning room. Then come the final steps of banding the cigar and packaging it. These final steps are overseen by the *escogedor*, who is responsible for classing the cigars by their respective tints so as to assure a certain homogeneity for each box. He or she is capable of distinguishing with the naked eye sixty-five different color nuances common to the outer wrapper. These include the whole spectrum of tints from green to black including the well-known browns: claro (tawny), colorado (reddish-brown) and maduro (dark brown).

In Cuba, the Havana and the revolution have not always gotten along together. At one point it even seemed possible that the Havana would disappear from the face of the earth! But reason and sense quickly got the upper hand, with over $400 million in revenue coming in after a good year. It is a lucrative cash crop on which Cuba depends. When he came to power in 1959, Castro immediately set about nationalizing the tobacco industry in Cuba, placing it under the control of the powerful State national tobacco company, Cubatabaco. In the

*The **vistas** (above), **which are found on the inside covers of the boxes. They are printed by the national printing press of Havana, which also prints the logos represented on the bands** (opposite page).*

*(Below) **Once finished, the cigars are stored for four to eight weeks in large cedar cabinets in the middle of the conditioning rooms, the **escarpates**, where they will lose the excess humidity acquired during their manufacturing. These **escarpates** can hold up to eighteen thousand cigars.***

same spirit, he initially decreed the suppression of all of the historical brands, viewing them as symbols of the decadent old regime. A single cigar brand, the Siboney, was substituted for the nine hundred and sixty different brands extant at the time. Only four different types of the Siboney were available, making this transformation of the Cuban tobacco industry truly astonishing. The results were catastrophic for the Cuban economy. The Siboney, symbol of the revolution, was rejected out of hand by foreign consumers, and export sales collapsed. Matters worsened in 1962 following the American blockade of Cuba, which froze all commerce between the two countries. This was a

A galera (gallery) photographed in 1918, with the cigar rollers seated side by side in front of their workbenches. Notice in the rear the "reader": an innovation dating from 1865 that was meant to entertain the rollers as they worked with readings from newspapers and novels. Today, the reader has been downsized for the most part in favor of the radio.

major setback since up until that time eighty-five percent of Cuban tobacco exports were destined for the United States. By abolishing the Havana, Castro had inadvertently banished the customer. This mistake was quickly recognized and there was a sudden sea change in the Cuban attitude towards ideological purity. In 1965, all of the historical brands were reissued, partly under the tutelege of Zino Davidoff, the celebrated Swiss tobacco merchant. Cuba counted on Europe from then on as its largest foreign market, with Spain, traditionally the second-largest consumer of Havanas, being its foremost client, followed by France, Switzerland and England. The Castro regime, in an attempt to control the damage done by the Siboney, began offering top of the line Havanas, and these "castricized" cigars currently

surpass their historical predecessors in terms of quality. Cohiba, a cigar that is one hundred percent "castricized," was initiated in 1968 and is acclaimed by Cubans to be among the best in the world. The quality of Cuban cigars on the whole continued to improve over the next two decades. Since 1990, howerer, Cuba has been living through dark times and near economic chaos following the collapse of the socialist regimes of the Eastern bloc countries. The continuing economic slide of the country has naturally hit the Havana hard, with production falling to approximately half what it was a few years earlier (production dropped from one hundred and twenty million cigars in 1987 to fifty-five million in 1994). This drop in production is largely due to a chronic shortage of fertilizer. This has made it impossible for Cuba to satisfy foreign demand, with demand rising in Spain alone by ninety million Havanas. The problem is still worsening. Cuba has attempted to stave off disaster since 1995 by proposing to its principal trading partners, the Tabacalera of Spain and the Seita of France, commercial agreements for assisting Cuba. As a result of these agreements, Tabacalera and Seita have financed improvements in the growing and harvesting of tobacco on the island in exchange for guarantees on the supply of cigars (six million units are accorded to France annually). This salvaging operation has permitted Cubans to achieve a near normal level of production, which is today at one hundred million cigars.

Today, Cubans still consider their tobacco products to be the best. Nevertheless, there remains stiff competition among the major producers of top quality cigars. The more serious rivals are the Dominican Republic and Honduras. There is of course an obvious explanation for the challenge presented by these countries to Cuban supremacy. The major Cuban cigar producers fled to these countries after the revolution, bringing with them the superior Cuban seeds and their expertise. This is the case of the Menendez family, dispossessed of H. Upmann and Montecristo, or the Cifuentes, the former owners of Partagas. Even though their cigars cannot compare with the originals, these families are determined to wage an unrelenting trade war against their Cuban counterparts. Thus, the international market has been bombarded by Dominican-made H. Upmann, by Honduran Romeo y Julieta and Mexican Sancho Panza.

There are even brands such as La Gloria Cubana manufactured in Miami. This situation has led to a legal imbroglio in which Cuba is deeply entangled, at risk of losing possession of a few of the most prestigious brands. Montecristo is a prickly case in point. Even if an experienced cigar consumer can tell the difference between an original Havana and one of its "evil twins," Cuba is not taking any chances on the market, and so has resorted to stamping each product with as many as five different brand labels, the most famous being the green seal that is the Cuban government's warranty for cigars exported from Havana.

The other challenge facing the Cuban tobacco industry is, of course, the free market, composed of a public with changing tastes and new demands to which the Havana must adapt. There has been in the last twenty years an irresistible trend toward the consumption of lighter tobaccos. This trend has altered the terrain significantly, even if some brands remain within the great tradition of the full-bodied Havana, for example, Romeo y Julieta, Bolivar and Ramon Allones, just to name a few of the unchanged old guard. Others have been modified and new brands have been created to satisfy the increasing demand for lighter and lighter cigars, at the risk, naturally, of offending purists among the consumers. And that's not all. Even the shape of the Havana has mutated and evolved to adapt to the changing market environment of the last twenty years, though some might argue that market forces have gone too far and fixed what wasn't broken, effectively mutilating what for centuries had been the preferred forms. Indeed, the result has been a standardization of the cigar form with the consequence that of the nine hundred and fifty former formats registered in manufacturers' catalogues, hardly seventy-two are still in production today, and only forty-two hand-rolled formats are available at all. Truly, imagination has all but gone out of the cigar with only Partagas still producing the amazing culebras, three cigars intertwined and bound together by a silk ribbon. And so goes the Koh-i-Noor, once produced by Henry Clay, now extinct, all 18 inches of it—a true dinosaur to say the least. Today, the largest Cuban models produced are a mere 9 1/2 inches in comparison. These are the especiales, followed in size by the prominentes weighing in at 8 inches, the churchills at 6 3/4 inches and the lonsdales at 6 1/4 inches. Nevertheless, it still takes a good two

Viva Cuaba

The rumor had been circulating for a long time that the Cubans were up to something. Only the happy day and the name of the newcomer remained unknown.
This was the Cuaba, introduced in November of 1996 and released on the international market with great fanfare. Despite the similar sounding name, the Cuaba was not intended to be a rival to the Cohiba, which remains today the standard bearer of Cuban cigars. All the same, the two brands do share the same remarkable aromatic qualities, and both do equal honor to the manufacturer La Laguito. The Cuaba are currently available in four figurado formats. Another addition followed in 1997: the Robaina, available in five formats: the Don Alejandro (double corona), the Unicos (torpedo), the Famosos (robusto), the Classico (lonsdale) and the Familiar (corona).

to three hours to reduce one of these models to ash. Alas, the average consumer today is a man, or woman, in a hurry, whose preferences tend naturally to the smaller models, from the coronas at 5 1/2 inches, perhaps the most popular model in the world, to the elegant cigarittos at just 4 inches (widely responsible for the induction of women into the world of the Havana).

Bolivar

The Bolivar was introduced in 1901 by the firm La Rocha in Havana. The cigar was named Bolivar in honor of the great revolutionary Simon Bolivar, who at the beginning of the last century led a number of insurrections to liberate the countries of Latin America from Spanish domination. Cuba itself ironically did not achieve independence from Spain until 1898, after four hundred years under the Spanish yoke. The insurrection began in 1895 and, lasting three years, was hard won. The *tabaqueros,* employees of the cigar manufacturers, played a crucial role in the liberation of their country. Indeed, the insurrection was initially fomented among their ranks; and history would have it that the call to battle, sounded by José Martí from Florida, came to them hidden in a cigar. The Bolivar was an immediate success with cigar lovers and was highly esteemed among the more full-bodied Havanas, having the rich, strong flavor that was preferred in those days. The French writer Eugène Marsan, author of a celebrated book on cigars, had no hesitation in recommending the Barons and Little Dukes of the Bolivar line to his readers, hailing them among a select class of "irreproachable" cigars. The Bolivar had its place among the best Havanas of its day, comparable to brands such as Henry Clay, Flor de Cuba, Corona and Villar y Villar. The zenith of its popularity did not come until the 1950's when the Cifuentes family took charge of its production. The Cifuentes, already the holders of Partagas, Ramon Allones, La Intimidad and some twenty other lesser-known brands, propelled the Bolivar to new heights of commercial success through clever marketing in conjunction with the family's better-known brands. Today, the Bolivar is still true to its traditional qualities. These robust Havanas are unmatched for their bold flavor, with the exception perhaps of Romeo y Julieta or the Escepción. More than twenty models are currently available on the market. Quite a few of these, however, are of an inferior quality, mechanically crafted and altogether disappointing. This leaves only a few great handmade models, which fortunately suffice to sustain the reputation of the Bolivar. The tradition of the large caliber cigar has been scrupulously maintained through the production of two stupendous churchills, the Inmensas and the Coronas Gigantes. Also to be noted are the Coronas Extra (gran corona) and the Inmensas (lonsdale) which figure among the best of the Bolivars. The Gold Medal, another lonsdale, is readily identified by the gold wrapper extending half the length of the cigar. The Bolivar has also created the smallest model on the market, the Delgado, a très petit corona only 1 1/2 inches long, that is not longer available. The trend toward lighter tobacco has led Bolivar to create a new series of models that are more subtly flavored and more accessible to the novice smoker. Among these models are the Especiales (gran panetela) and the Royal Corona (robusto), which was originally named the Prince Charles. Since 1983, General Cigar has held the commercial rights on the American market to the Bolivar. However, the brand is not currently in production. The rights were acquired from Ramon Cifuentes, the last private owner of a cigar brand in Havana before his exile from Cuba after the Revolution.

Bolivar: a must among the full-bodied Havanas.
To be enjoyed in the format either of the Coronas
Gigantes, the Inmensas or the Coronas Extra.

5 1/2 inches

52 ring gauge

Belicosos Finos

This torpedo is perhaps not the most representative of the Bolivar, but it is without doubt one of the rare Havanas that can claim to be a true rival of Montecristo No. 2. Full bodied like most formats of the brand, it exudes among the most pronounced and complex of aromas and is much appreciated and well-known among the initiated. This is one of the most beautifully constructed cigars and a real pleasure to smoke. It has written its own chapter in the history of the Havana.

Cohiba

As far as the people of the socialist republic of Cuba are concerned, only two things are certain: death and the excellence of their Cohibas. They believe this with such conviction that they hardly question the quality of even the first brand, the Siboney, created just after the revolution—that showcase production of "castricism" in the matter of top-quality cigars—and it's no wonder, given their long-restricted choices in tobacco matters. The original Cohiba revolutionary models were concocted under the aegis of Ernesto "Che"

themselves—an effective way of assuring their notoriety. Castro himself was a great help in that regard, never parting in public from his Lanceros (7 1/2 inches long), which became "the cigar of El Lider Massimo." In short, before their commercialization in 1982, nearly everybody had heard about the Cohibas and was eager to try them. The success following their introduction was immediate. Marketing genius apart, these are top of the line cigars, full bodied, aromatic and manufactured with the greatest care and scrupulous attention to detail. The tobaccos used to make Cohibas come from ten different plantations resulting in a rich blend. Three to six of these—the best—are used for each line of production the following year. Cohibas are manufactured by El Laguito, which is reputed to recruit the most proficient *torcedores* in the land. Here the different tobaccos are under constant quality control from a team of six samplers who examine them at the end of the production line. Two new series will see the light of day—those with the marked qualities required for a lighter cigar, in accord with the new public taste. The year of 1989, for instance, saw the introduction of the Linea classica, with the Esplendidos (churchill), Robustos (robusto) and Exquisitos (panetela). The year 1992 saw the launching of the Linea 1992, so christened in honor of the five hundredth anniversary of Christopher Columbus' discovery of Cuba. Five different

Guevara, then minister of industry for the new socialist republic. If Che considered the cigar to be the "indispensable companion of the revolutionary," it was to his advantage to stay in the good graces of his foreign clientele. They were not about to buy the Siboney, that singular cigar that Castro had tried to impose upon them. Che took the matter in hand, knowing well that there is nothing like competition to bring out the best, and set about selecting the most promising Havana specialists, like Avelino Lara, who headed the selection committee and later became director of the manufacturer El Laguito. Also to emerge at the top was Eduardo Rivero, of Por Larrañaga, who created the famous Lanceros in 1963. The first three models went into production in 1968. They were the Lanceros (gran panetela), the Coronas Especiales (corona) and the Panetelas (a cigarrito in spite of its name). Up until 1982, they were exclusively reserved for VIPs of the regime and the bosses of the brands

models of the Linea 1992 are available, the aptly named Siglo 1 (a très petit corona), Siglo II (another petit corona), Siglo III (a corona), IV (a large corona) and Siglo V (a lonsdale). The appearance of the Siglo may have been related to the sudden change made in 1990 by Zino Davidoff in favor of cigars from the Dominican Republic. Previous models had been made by El Laguito since 1969, and the great Davidoff may have taken umbrage at the preference the Cubans showed toward their Cohibas as far as the choice of the best tobaccos were concerned.

Cohiba means tobacco in the language of the Tainos. Since 1968, the brand has been synonymous with the "best cigar in the world," as far as Cubans are concerned, with such outstanding models as the Lanceros, the Esplendidos and the Robustos.

Esplendidos

*If Cohiba represents
all that is finest in Cuban
craftsmanship,
this churchill is one of its
masterpieces. Living up
to its name, the Esplendidos
expresses perhaps even
better than the Robustos
or the Lanceros—themselves
equally prized—what could
be called the culture
of Cohiba. Fairly full-bodied,
well-balanced, robust yet
cool, and of an excellent
construction, this cigar
is unanimously appreciated
in political, artistic
and business circles.
It is on the verge
of becoming a sign
of distinction and
commands a cult following.*

7 inches

47 ring gauge

Fonseca

onseca is an old brand name first registered in Havana in the last century. Its creator was F.E. Fonseca, whose portrait is still visible on the cigar box covers. He is dressed in the habit of the colonial period as a *marquista,* or marquis. This member of the landed classes was of Spanish origin and, among others, played a crucial role in launching a revolution in cigars during the 1830's. These mavericks of the day were no longer satisfied by merely supplying the manufacturers with tobacco. They opened up factories and literally staked their own names, as well as the respective brand names, on the quality of the cigars themselves. Naturally, the brand name became something of a coat of arms, and Fonseca has maintained this aristocratic style to this day. As pointed out on the cigar box itself, the tobacco used for manufacturing these cigars always comes from the best soil of the Vuelta Abajo region— *con las mejores vegas de Vuelta Abajo.* A blend of very smooth tobaccos gives to these Havanas a particularly light character, a character that is the hallmark of the brand. The only blemish on the coat of arms is the growing recourse to mechanical manufacturing exemplified by the disappointing Delicias. There remain three impeccable models *hecho a mano.* The Fonseca No. 1 (lonsdale) is at the summit of the mild Havana, with the Cosacos (corona) and the Invictos (figurado) just a step behind. The smallest format of the series is the Kdt Cadetes (4 1/2 inches long), which is much less satisfying than the three others. The presentation of the cigars is elegant and meticulous. Each cigar is wrapped in silver foiled paper and then covered by a fine white sheet of paper. The effect is altogether reminiscent of the milky light reflected off the cotton tarpaulined *vegas* of the Vuelta Abajo.

5 1/4 inches

Cosacos

Among Fonseca's four handmade formats that remain true to the Havana tradition, the Cosacos is the best. Like other Fonseca cigars, the Cosacos come wrapped in white paper. Beginners will note the mildness, the discreet aroma and the freshness of this corona. If properly smoked, slowly and at the right burning temperature, the Cosacos is thoroughly enjoyable.

40 ring gauge

LA GLORIA CUBANA

HABANA

The brand was then placed in the hands of Partagas, which at the time had the ambition of commercializing a cigar with a more subtle flavor. This was in keeping with the new public tastes to which Partagas wished to appeal, though not at the expense of its reputation as one of the leading full-bodied Havanas. Of course, La Gloria Cubana cigars are rolled by the manufacturer Francisco Perez German alongside those of Partagas. The series currently includes only nine models, four of which are grouped together in the Gold Medal series. The Gold Medal No. 1 is a gran panetela, Gold Medal No. 2 is a churchill, and No. 3 and No. 4 are both panetelas. The Tainos, a churchill, is in a class of its own. Its name honors the Tainos Indians, the first cigar smokers in history, whom Columbus encountered when he landed in Cuba in 1492.

It should be noted that Gloria Cubana cigars have been manufactured in Miami since 1972 by the company El Credito Cigar, and in the Dominican Republic since 1995. They are readily identifiable by their maduro (brown-black) wrapper.

La Gloria Cubana was created in the last century by Juan Francisco Rocha. The brand had its place in the sun for a certain period of time, but was eclipsed following the 1959 revolution. La Gloria Cubana was not the only brand to find itself in this lamentable position. Such historic brands as Villar y Villar, Cabanas, La Corona—and most notably, Henry Clay, whose principal sin was to have been a brand name honoring a statesman and orator from the United States— were relegated to obscurity. None of these brands would ever regain favor among the members of the new regime— except La Gloria Cubana, which reappeared during the 1970's.

LA GLORIA CUBANA DE C. E. G. HABANA

After a long absence, the "Glory of Cuba" is once again a star on the Havana stage. The different formats clearly merit their star status: from the Gold Medal to the Tainos, and also including the Cetros, the Sabrosos, the Tapados and the Minutos.

Tainos

The customary comparison of this brand to the Partagas line is entirely justified, especially since the two brands have become closely linked. Less full-bodied and easier to smoke than the Partagas, the different formats offered by La Gloria Cubana are intended for a less mainstream—though not necessarily less demanding—clientele. More than the other formats, this churchill represents the brand's concern for quality. Of a robust but subtle and smooth character, the Tainos has a rich and woody taste and can hold its own with respect to other brands of the same format. A good choice among the choicest of cigars in the world.

7 inches

47 ring gauge

Hoyo de Monterrey

Gener was producing. His goal in introducing this new brand was to capitalize on the initial success of La Escepción. In the United States as in Europe, Hoyo de Monterrey rapidly acquired a reputation for being the lightest and smoothest of the Havanas. The success of the cigar was converted into its own promotional pitch when Gener began printing the initials of its most illustrious patrons on the cigar band itself. Gener gained total control over the business after 1870 and remained in control until his death in 1900. His factory was at the time one of the largest in Cuba, employing no fewer than three hundred and fifty rollers and producing more than fifty million cigars a year. His descendants, however, were less visionary and less driven. Shortly after the death of Gener, they would abandon the tobacco industry altogether in favor of sugar cane. The brand was then bought by Ramon Fernandez and Fernando Palicio, co-owners of Punch and Belinda. They went on to develop in the 1930's the most prestigious models of Hoyo de Monterrey. Quite naturally, it was to the owners of Hoyo de Monterrey whom Zino Davidoff would turn in 1947 to launch the legendary Châteaux series of cigar. These cigars were made of the best tobacco from Hoyo de Monterrey and manufactured to Davidoff's standards. Today, the brand is still counted among the finest of the smoother cigars, with fifteen or so handmade models currently available (the line itself includes approximately thirty formats). The larger formats were initially the hallmark of the brand, notably the Particulares, an

The brand Hoyo de Monterrey, introduced in 1867, is the creation of José Gener, one of the great barons of the tobacco industry who built his fortune not only in tobacco but also in sugar cane. Gener was born in Spain and emigrated to Cuba in 1831 at the age of thirteen. He was apprenticed to his uncle, Miguel Jané y Gener, who owned a tobacco plantation in the Vuelta Abajo and sold a small brand of cigar, the Majagua, on the local market. José Gener, however, saw the larger potential of this trade, and had bigger ideas in mind than his uncle. In 1851, Gener

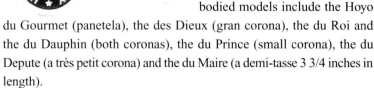

especial at 9 1/2 inches in length, the Double Coronas, the Churchills, and the Epicures No. 1 and No 2 (a gran corona and a robusto, respectively). The Hoyo, a sub-brand, appeared in 1970, enlarging the series with the addition of smaller-sized models. Six fuller-bodied models include the Hoyo

persuaded his uncle to open a factory in Havana. There, he created a new brand called La Escepción, with which he intended to target the huge American market. It was an immediate success. Gener personally controlled the entire line of production from the plantation to the manufacturer and acquired an invaluable experience in the production and marketing of cigars. He used the proceeds of this initial success to buy up the best farm land in the Vuelta Abajo, notably the land around San Juan y Martinez. This is where, in 1860, he acquired the Hoyo de Monterrey plantation. Seven years after this acquisition, the name Hoyo de Monterrey was used to commercialize the new brand of cigar that

du Gourmet (panetela), the des Dieux (gran corona), the du Roi and the du Dauphin (both coronas), the du Prince (small corona), the du Depute (a très petit corona) and the du Maire (a demi-tasse 3 3/4 inches in length).

From one of the most famous plantations in the Vuelta Abajo was born a brand noted for being among the smoothest of the Havanas. Some of the best formats are the Churchills, the Epicure No. 1, the Exquisitos, the Hoyo du Gourmet and the Double Coronas.

du Gourmet
HABANA
MONTERREY
de
OSÉ GENER
HABANA
LE HOYO
du Gourmet

Double Coronas

Belonging to one of the best formats available on the market, after the especiales, this double corona has a charming mildness and a smooth if somewhat sweet taste. Like all the other formats of the brand Hoyo de Monterrey, this cigar is notable for its subtle and light smoking qualities. Only its equivalent from Punch and, perhaps to a different extent, the Lusitanias of Partagas, can compare in terms of quality.

7 1/2 inches

49 ring gauge

H. Upmann

Herman Upmann was an English banker who, since the 1830's, had the habit of importing from Cuba excellent Havanas emblazoned with his name, which he then graciously bestowed upon his clients. Their popularity was such that he undertook the making of the cigars himself and so was born the trademark H. Upmann in 1844. Upmann's move into the manufacturing of cigars was timely since the bank was to fail shortly thereafter, leaving Herman Upmann closed in banking but still holding the cigars. True to the English love of tradition, H. Upmann never wavered from the established English taste for strong, full-bodied Havanas, innovating models that rarely varied from the originals. The celebrity of these cigars only grew over the course of the nineteenth century, and a whole harvest of gold medals was reaped at many different expositions (seven in all between the years 1865 and 1893). These successes boosted the status of the H. Upmann cigar into the upper and most exclusive rungs of society, where they were enjoyed not only in Britain but elsewhere. Thus, H. Upmann basked in the privilege of being King Alfonso XII's titled purveyor, and the Spanish king indulged Herman with the right to use the royal coat of arms on the H. Upmann boxes. His cigar factory in Havana was one of the largest in the country. It was included among the so-called "first class" factories such as Partagas and Hoyo de Monterrrey, which indicates that it employs more than fifty laborers. At the top of the class was the manufacturer Cabanas y Cabajol, which employed only thirteen laborers in 1833 but counted over two thousand among its ranks by 1886. H. Upmann would launch a veritable revolution in the transport and distribution of cigars to Europe. He was one of the first to use cedar boxes to store and transport cigars. Before him, the custom of the time was to bundle the cigars in units of fifty to a hundred. From then on, the connoisseur could enjoy a cigar almost as fresh and moist as if it had just left the manufacturer. That put an end to the dry Havana, which was usually rehumidified by a lick of the tongue just prior to lighting up, a dubious custom that persists to this day despite the fact that it serves no practical purpose. Later, H. Upmann would lead the field once again by introducing the first cigar models to be conserved in aluminum tubes. In 1936, the brand H. Upmann reached a turning point. It was bought out by the Menendez and Garcia families, who already owned Montecristo and soon would own Por Larrañaga. This made them the largest producers of Havanas in the world with twenty-five million cigars produced each year, all brands included. Since the 1959 revolution, the manufacturer H. Upmann, since rechristened José Martí, has been in charge of making the original models; it produces, among others, Montecristo and the Cohibas. The brand is still a favorite among aficionados for its strong-flavored and full-bodied Havanas. Some forty different models are available, but a lot of them are machine made. The larger models are to be preferred, notably two stout churchills: the Sir Winston (as it deserves to be named) and the Monarchs, conserved in an aluminum tube. Tradition notwithstanding, the brand has known how to follow the trends of the times and offers light models such as the Connoisseur No. 1 (a robusto) and the Cristales (a corona), the last Havanas still delivered in glass canisters.

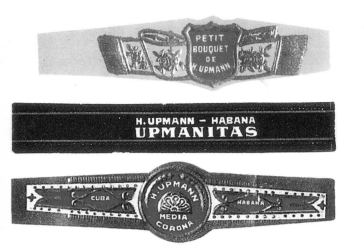

H. Upmann, master of the "chair leg" format, distinguished by their strong, harsh aromas. The churchills, Sir Winston and the Monarchs, are perfect for the smoker who enjoys the more pungent varieties.

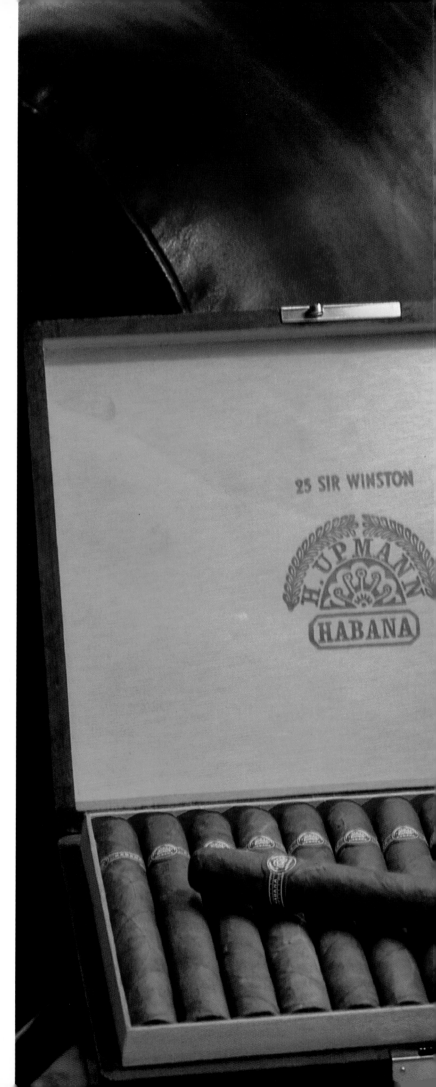

Sir Winston

*It goes without saying
that the Sir Winston is
a churchill. It is the most
full-bodied of the churchills
and often the choice of those
who prefer stronger cigars
with a blunt and
pronounced aroma.
The Havana diehards will
find in this cigar the great
tradition of Cuban
craftsmanship. It is a
diehard itself, as newer
products from other lands
reach the market to satisfy
the trend toward more
and more refined tastes.*

7 inches

47 ring gauge

Juan Lopez

The brand name Flor de Juan Lopez was registered in Havana at the end of the last century by the firm Juan Lopez y Cia. The boxes hardly let slip the consumer's attention that the brand won first prize at the Cuban national exposition in 1911. This is a charming touch of modesty given the truckloads of gold medals garnered from World Expos by such brands as H. Upmann and Romeo y Julieta. The brand has had a poor distribution on the European market for quite a long time. That in part is due to the low production volume—a consequence of the slow and careful manufacturing of these cigars. This simply means that the house of Flor de Juan Lopez still continues in the old tradition of the small manufacturer, and so there is no mechanical rolling, no bottom line approaches to production, and no cutting corners in the workshops of this maker of fine cigars. Indeed, each cigar is *totalmente hecho a mano* according to the strictest criteria of the artisans. The series has an almost private character, with only six models registered in the catalogue. These cigars are made with tobacco from the Vuelta Abajo, and are among the milder Havanas available on the market. To the experienced Havana smoker, they may be even a bit too mild. For those consumers who are part of the trend favoring milder tobacco, however, this is a brand to be preferred—as much for its mildness as for the elegant forms of the different models. For the most part, the brand has given more weight to the medium- and smaller-sized models, with the Selección No. 1, a gran corona 5 1/2 long, and the Patricias, a très petit corona 4 1/2 long, being the most notable. Don't pass over the following: the Coronas, the Petit Coronas and the Selección No 2 (a robusto). Supremely refined, the Selección No. 1 and No. 2 (a robusto) are presented in boxes of twenty-five with a sliding cover.

4 7/8 inches

50 ring gauge

Selección No. 2

This cigar is increasing in popularity among those who prefer its short, thick-set format made in the great Havana tradition. This robusto and the gran corona Juan Lopez, are the most recent additions to a selection of formats that has changed little—a selection that has, however, never failed to please its most devoted clients. Both are at the top of the line offered by this historical brand. The robusto is smooth and light, very aromatic though perhaps a bit green. It makes for a pleasant afternoon smoke after lunch or between meals. Of a subtle, well-balanced construction, it deserves to be compared to more commercially prominent cigars such as the Epicure No. 2 by Hoyo, the Robustos by Cohiba or the Special R by Davidoff.

Montecristo

The Montecristos have won it all, every prize and trophy, since their creation. They have the reputation of being the best cigars in the world, the most widely sold and the most often imitated. The last twenty years, however, have somewhat recolored the truth, and the Montecristos are now struggling to live up to their reputation. More and more connoisseurs of the Havana are turning their noses up at the vaunted Montecristos. The brand was launched in 1935 by the Menendez and Garcia families. These two families had united twelve years earlier to create their first line of cigar, the Particulares, which they sold locally. The Montecristo was born of the two families' expertise, with the intention of opening up the international market to them. They therefore promoted the Montecristo as a cigar of prestige, with the first five models innovatively named: No. 1, 2, 3, 4 and 5. Their success in the United States was such that the name Montecristo soon became associated in the consumer's mind with the five finest cigars available. To count them off from the beginning, the Montecristo No. 1 is a strong lonsdale formerly in vogue among the mighty of Wall Street. The No. 2 is a smooth, slightly sweet figurado. The No. 3 is a larger caliber corona and No. 4 and No. 5 are a petit and très petit corona, respectively. Riding the wave of their success, the firm of Menendez y Garcia soon bought out the companies of H. Upmann and Por Larrañaga, thus metamorphosing from 1939 on into the largest cigar-producers in Cuba. They were beached however by the revolution, which chased them into exile twenty years later. The families are still contesting the Lider Massimo's right to use the Montecristo name and have attempted to take the biscuit from him by fabricating cigars with such subtly veiled brand names as the Montecruz (today made in the Dominican Republic). Despite the adversity, the Montecristo would dominate the market into the 1980's. Naturally, the Cubans accorded them special status, for these cigars were the showcase brand of their craftsmanship—a privilege that would eventually be given to the Cohiba in 1982. Montecristos are smooth, mild cigars, and the most subtle blends of tobacco are used in their production. No fewer than four different varieties of leaf are used, as opposed to the normal three. They also have the advantage of being produced by the best manufacturers, like Jose Marti (H. Upmann), Francisco Perez German (Partagas) or El Laguito. In the early 1970's, four new models appeared: the Montecristo A (an especial 9 1/2 inches long), the Montecristo Especiales (gran panetela), the Especiales No. 2 (corona) and the Joyitas (demitasse). Finally, the series was further expanded by the aptly named Montecristo B (petit corona) and the Montecristo Tubos, a lonsdale conserved in an aluminum tube (hence the name "Tubos"). The standard series recently expanded with the addition of No. 6 and No. 7, both of limited production. Those were the glory days of Montecristo when their success seemed universal. Even today they comprise half of the annual Havana sales, or, to put it more discreetly, the modest sum of $200 million. Unfortunately, the volume of production of this famous brand has not stopped growing, all seemingly at the expense of the cigar's quality and taste. This is also true of the historic models, such as the Montecristo No. 3 and 4 which continue to proliferate as the world's most widely sold cigars even though they are but shadows of what they once had been. Only the large models continue to satisfy the connoisseur as much as they do the public's demand, and the Montecristo A remains, whatever the case against it may be, one of the very great Havanas.

Montecristo is still an elite brand, which displeases the purists who reproach it for its inconsistency in terms of quality. The Montecristo A is quite simply the best, and the No. 2 is well worthwhile.

6 1/8 inches

52 ring gauge

No. 2

Few cigars elicit as much appreciation or controversy as this classic. It is the figurado of figurados to its advocates. But it burns too readily and lacks subtlety as far as its detractors are concerned. In fact, if subtlety is not its strong point, it has an avid following by virtue of its strength and robustness. The quality is uneven and varies from shipment to shipment, making it in a way a victim of the brand's overall success. Its strong taste and tendency to burn quickly can take the uninitiated by surprise. Enjoy with moderation and beware of counterfeits.

Partagas

La Flor de Tabacos de Partagas appeared in the brand name registry in 1845. Its creator, Don Jaime Partagas, of Catalan origin, was the owner of a small tobacco factory in Havana in 1827. He had the ambition from the beginning to engage in the larger scale production of cigars, but lacked the capital to launch himself into the big leagues. While biding his time, he judiciously purchased different plantations in the Vuelta Abajo region. It took him twenty years before he was able to interest investors in the project. Once he had the backing, he created the company La Flor de Tabacos de Partagas y Cia. The brand is reputed among the stronger Havanas with very full-bodied aromas. The quality of the tobacco is exceptional, since Don Jaime Partagas was one of the first to devote meticulous attention to the techniques of product improvement, notably in the area of fermentation. The factory where the cigars are made is in the Calle de la Industria in a sumptuous colonial style building. It is still there today and, despite a renovation in 1987, remains the oldest cigar factory standing in Havana. It is also one of Havana's most popular tourist attractions and, for the cigar aficionado, a must see. It was inside these walls about 1865 that a new form of *tabaquero* appeared. This was the "reader," who held the important job of reading aloud to the rollers from newspapers and novels while they worked. The reader's first appearance on the scene was warmly appreciated by the laborers and was eventually seen as something of a social and cultural right. The importance of the role played by the reader can only be underlined by noting his continuing presence in the factories, even in the face of that high-tech competitor for his job—the radio. In 1864, Don Jaime tragically died from an assassin's bullet at one of his plantations in the Vuelta Abajo. The brand was then picked up by the banker José Bances, who would do much to enlarge the cigar's popularity. This included winning a coveted gold medal at the World Expo in Paris in 1879. In 1900, he was obliged to give up the business, and it passed into the hands of Ramon Cifuentes Llano and José Fernandez. The latter would soon retire, leaving Partagas entirely to the Cifuentes family, who would maintain sole possession of it until the 1959 revolution. Today, Partagas has the largest series of models of any of the Havana brands, with more than forty models registered in the catalogue. Most of these models, however, are machine made and intended, like the Chicos, for a non-demanding clientele. That leaves some twenty superior models, like the Lusitanias, a double corona 7 3/4 inches in length and the Shorts, a très petit corona 4 inches long. Special mention should be made of the stunning culebras—three cigars twisted together—which only Partagas and H. Upmann continue to make. After the revolution, the Partagas manufacturer was renamed Francisco Perez German. The two hundred rollers employed here can produce in a good year as many as eight million cigars. That means that Partagas alone accounts for nearly half of the manufacturer's total cigar production in Havana. The other half is divided among five other brands: Bolivar, Ramon Allones, La Gloria Cubana, Cohiba and Montecristo.

The old Partagas factory is the most visited in Havana, and the brand itself still offers some of the most satisfying of the full-bodied puros. Among Partagas' best: the Presidentes, the Lusitanias, and the 8-9-8 Varnished.

8-9-8 Varnished

Full-bodied, aromatically rich and possessing a frank and spicy flavor, this churchill is the most sought-after of the Partagas among the top of the line cigars, with the exception of the Lusitanias. The Varnished, whose name derives from the presentation of three layers of 8 cigars followed by 9 and then 8 again, has enjoyed substantial commercial success. The same packaging is found in Cuba at Ramon Allones, in the Dominican Republic at Ashton and Cuesta Rey and in Jamaica (8-9-8 Collection). Its box of varnished wood and rounded sides has also played a role in its success. This 8-9-8 is not to be confused with the other Partagas 8-9-8, the 8-9-8 Cabinet, which is a gran corona, somewhat easier to smoke and somewhat smaller. It comes in a box of non-varnished wood.

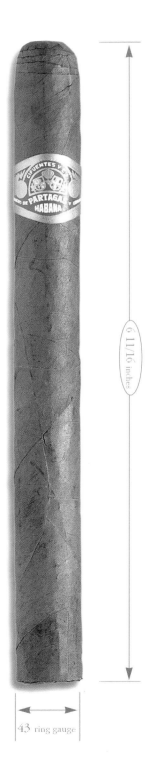

6 11/16 inches

43 ring gauge

Punch

Punch was established in 1840 by a German industrialist named Stockmann. The name comes from the well-known English satirical magazine of the same era. The choice of this name reveals the clear intention of Stockmann to target initially the English market. Punch is the oldest existing brand of Havana with the exception of

MANUEL LOPEZ

Por Larrañaga, which was created in 1834, and Ramon Allones, which dates from 1837. Despite the fact that the English had already put their colonial holdings to the business of manufacturing cigars (such as Macanudo and Temple Hall during the last century), they nevertheless remained devoted to the original Havanas of a fuller-bodied, more pungent appeal. The robust flavor of Punch would be the hallmark of the first formats. In 1884, the brand was bought by Juan Valle y Cia, a company in which he was to play a decisive role. He would preside over its destiny until his death in 1925. His name is honored on the cigar bands to this day. In the 1930's, the brand would fall under the dominion of Ramon Fernandez and Fernando Palicio, who held onto it until the revolution. These two were already in possession of Hoyo de Monterrey and knew how to bestow upon Punch the qualities of sweetness and light which

still characterize the brand. Today, the different models are rolled by Fernando Roig and company (ex-La Corona), one of the six principal manufacturers in Havana today. The House proposes a particularly extensive series of models from the Diademas Extra, an especial 9 1/4 inches long, to the Petit Punch, a très petit corona 4 inches long. Indeed, Punch is, along with Partagas, the brand with the widest selection available. This line includes no fever than six gran coronas (among which are included the Black Prince, the Nectar No. 2 and the highly esteemed Punch-Punch), two churchills (the Churchills and the Monarcas), three panetelas (the Coronets, the Panetelas and the Punchinellos), and six petits coronas (including the excellent Coronations, Presidentes and Petit Coronas del Punch), all making for a grand total of forty different formats. Unfortunately, the brand does its name a disservice by manufacturing such machine-made models as the Palmas Reales. However, the apparent excess does not detract overall from the variety and diversity of aromas found in these cigars. It should be noted that since 1965 Punch has also been manufactured in Honduras by Villazon & Co., following the exile of the Palicio family after the 1959 revolution. Villazon has also acquired three other brands formerly owned by the Palicio family, namely: José Gener, Belinda and Hoyo de Monterrey (which offers

the most prestigious non-Cuban cigar in the world, the Hoyo de Monterrey Excalibur). The Honduran Punch are fuller-bodied than their Cuban homonyms, while the opposite is generally the case for other brands manufactured both inside Cuba and abroad. The non-Cuban Punch, like their Cuban siblings, enjoy an excellent reputation among havanophiles and cigar lovers in general, with such popular models such as the Grand Diademas and the Grand Cru series (Château Lafitte, Château Corona and Château Margaux).

Despite the name, Punch offers some of the lightest Havanas, well-balanced and remarkably smooth. These are good cigars for the novice to begin with, especially the Diademas Extra, the Punch-Punch and the Royal Coronation.

7 5/8 inches

49 ring gauge

Double Coronas

With a whole spectrum of formats on offer, Punch provides some of the best formats to choose from: the Punch-Punch de luxe, a gran corona; the Diademas Extra, an especial; the Royal Selection No. 12, a petit corona; or for those fonder of the smaller formats, the Petit Punch, a très petit corona. Nevertheless, it is without a doubt the Double Coronas that holds the ticket, a subtle blend of woody, earthy and spicy flavors. It is a well-constructed cigar, the expression itself of good taste. A delicious harmony of flavors. A magnificent cigar.

Rafael Gonzalez

A rich landowner from the Vuelta Abajo region introduced the world at the beginning of the century to the brand Flor de Rafael Gonzalez. He was Marquis Rafael Gonzalez. The business, at the time, was made up of artisans, and the Marquis' ambition did not extend beyond the local market. In 1928, the brand was taken over by two American businessmen who, with a large investment of capital, catapulted the brand onto the international market. This is just one example among many of an American takeover in the Cuban cigar industry of the early twentieth century. The tobacco consortium Tabacalera Americana would, itself, eventually control six important brands and numerous smaller ones. The United States became Cuba's principal trading partner following the 1898 revolution, and, through the creation of powerful trusts, would go on to control key sectors of the Cuban economy, especially those of tobacco and sugar. The Tobacco Trust at the time imported into the United States some two hundred and ninety-one different Cuban brands representing two hundred and fifty million cigars each year. Too tainted by its American association, the brand would disappear following the 1959 revolution, along with Henry Clay, of course. Nevertheless, the brand was re-released in the 1970's under the supervision of El Rey del Mundo. Rafael Gonzalez has since cultivated, in the manner of its master El Rey del Mundo, a cigar worthy of the great Cuban tradition, offering perhaps the most subtle and light of Havanas available today. Fifteen or so different models are noted in the catalogue, running the gamut from the Lonsdales (6 1/4 inches in length) to the elegant Panetelas (4 1/2 inches long) and the Cigarritos (4 1/2 inches).

Coronas Extra

This cigar is a favorite for its mildness, delicate gingerbread flavor and characteristically "green" aroma, which recalls the days when the various formats were differentiated by the green tints of their respective wrappers. Mildness here means a light, honeyed taste. This gran corona is a bit more boldly accented and stronger than the other Rafael Gonzaleses. It is the best of the brand, in part because of its elegant and solid construction.

5 5/8 inches

46 ring gauge

LA BOÎTE

HABANA

THESE CIGARS HAVE BEEN MANUFACTURED FROM A SECRET BLEND OF PURE VUELTA ABAJO TOBACCOS SELECTED BY THE MARQUEZ RAFÆL GONZALEZ *Grandee of Spain*. FOR MORE THAN 20 YEARS THIS BLEND HAS EXISTED. IN ORDER THAT THE CONNOISSŒUR MAY FULLY APPRECIATE THE PERFECT FRAGRANCE THEY SHOULD BE SMOKED EITHER WITHIN ONE MONTH OF THE DATE OF SHIPMENT FROM HAVANA OR SHOULD BE CAREFULLY MATURED FOR ABOUT ONE YEAR.

Gonzalez

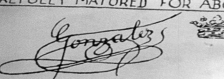

Ramon Allones

This brand was created in 1837 by Ramon Allones, a Spaniard from Galicia who emigrated to Cuba a few years earlier. The brand is one of the oldest existing brands along with Por Larrañaga (1834). Ramon Allones was the first to use the *vistas* to decorate the interior of the cigar box. These colored designs, often baroque in style, constitute a rich artistic patrimony that the Cubans have neglected for quite a long time now. However, the cigar boxes they adorn remain, like cigar bands themselves, much sought after collector's items, and are esteemed something of a prize among "vitophiles." Later, the company would introduce another innovation: the 8-9-8 format, so called because the cigars are presented in the box in a first layer of eight cigars followed by a layer of nine and topped off with a second layer of eight. The brand was bought out by the Cifuentes, already the owners of Partagas, in 1920. Ramon Allones thus found its place in the school of strong Havanas with its striking, full-bodied taste, which continues to assure its reputation. They are still manufactured along with Partagas, but contrary to the latter, these models are all rolled by hand. The larger models tend to be preferred by the experienced cigar smoker, such as the Coronas Gigantes (double corona) and the 8-9-8 Cabinet Selection Varnished, which is a churchill. Nonetheless, Ramon Allones is also much appreciated by a clientele who prefer the more modest models that are easier to smoke. To be recommended are the Coronas (5 1/2 inches) and the Ramonitas, a cigarrito 4 inches long but still very full-bodied.

Specially Selected

This very old brand excels in every format. Though the Coronas Gigantes (double corona) or the 8-9-8 Cabinet Selection Varnished (churchill) still encounter some criticism among the more selective smokers, the robusto Specially Selected is one of the outstanding examples of its format. Many connoisseurs would place it on the same rung as its rival from Cohiba. That says it all. It embraces all that is best in a robusto, uniting both woody and fruity aromas.

4 15/16 inches

50 ring gauge

El Rey del Mundo

In 1848, the registry of brand name Havanas was enlarged by the addition of two new brands: El Rey del Mundo and Sancho Panza. Both brands were owned by Emilio Ohmstedt, a merchant of German origin specializing in import-export. Ohmstedt had emigrated to Cuba seven years earlier. Registering a brand name became mandatory in 1848, as it was useful in keeping track of the number of different brands that were being commercialized. In 1848, there were a total of two hundred and thirty-two different cigar brands and some one hundred and eighty other brands commercializing cigarettes, none of which had existed prior to 1810. This was the golden age of the Havana, and it was to last throughout the entire nineteenth century. It was also the century of the tobacco baron, and names such as Jaime Partagas (Partagas) and José Gener (Hoyo de Monterrey) dominated the scene. Emilio Ohmstedt had every intention of profiting from this new prosperity. But his small factory on the Calle de los Angeles had a small production volume, and Emilio unfortunately was to die an untimely death in 1870 before witnessing the real success of his Havanas. The brands weren't resurrected until 1882 by the manufacturer Antonio Allones. Antonio Allones had the idea of placing a series of top-quality cigars on the international market with the name El Rey del Mundo (King of the World), naturally being the signature of their products. This was no idle fancy; and in their enthusiasm in conquering the market they even renamed the company "El Rey del Mundo Cigar Co." The return of the brand would be for good. The introduction of machine-made cigars, however, has only served to diminish the brand's reputation. El Rey del Mundo nevertheless has maintained a standard of quality that it lives up to today, and is a sure winner for its sweet accent and smoothness. The brand is represented by twenty different models. The Tainos (churchill) and the Lonsdales (lonsdale) are among the largest formats offered, and their remarkable mildness may make them a good introduction to these two formats with a reputation for being difficult to smoke. It should be noted that at least two hours are needed to properly smoke a churchill. The Choix Suprême is a short-butted robusto 5 inches long with a diameter that is a disproportional 3/4 inch. There is no other like it in the line. Among the small formats are a number of inviting choices, with the Demi-Tasse at 4 inches and the Senoritas of 4 1/2 inches—a diminutive mild cigar destined for an adventurous feminine clientele not yet ready for the more masculine Havanas. There is also a brand called El Rey del Mundo that is fabricated in Honduras by the firm Villazon & Co., which is owned by Dan Blumenthal and Frank Llaneza. Villazon & Co. bought the commercial rights for the brand in 1965 from the company Antonio, which was based in Tampa following the revolution. They also held the rights to Sancho Panza and Rafael Gonzales, also acquired at the same time by Villazon & Co. The Honduran El Rey del Mundo are very full-bodied cigars for hardier smokers, which makes it impossible to confuse them with their Cuban counterparts. The Honduran line is a large one with some thirty or so models; it nonetheless includes some light-bodied cigars, such as the very light Elegante, Tino and Reynita models.

Overstated perhaps as far as the name goes, the "King of the World" may be the king of the light cigars. The Tainos, the Isabel and the Choix Suprême are the perfect introduction to the Havana for the uninitiated.

FABRICA DE TABACOS
REY DEL MUNDO CIGAR CO.
PROVEEDOR DE LA REAL CASA
ESTABLECIDA EN 1848.
PADRE VARELA 852

EL REY DEL MUNDO

HABANA

El Rey del Mundo

Choix Suprême

It is part of a trinity along with the robustos of Cohiba and Ramon Allones. It can be considered the representative of its brand, with a mildness and lightness that appeals to both beginners and diehards alike. The El Rey del Mundo line has few detractors, but a certain over-refinement in its aroma might be mistaken for a lack of character. The Choix Suprême tempers that reproach with its robustness and pleasant burning qualities.

5 inches

49 ring gauge

Romeo y Julieta

The brand Romeo y Julieta was launched in 1850 by Inocencio Alvarez and Manin Garcia. The business has always had a reputation for craftsmanship about it which has made the brand a leading figure on the international market. It has won gold medal after gold medal at different international expositions from Antwerp (1885) to Paris (1889 and 1900) and Brussels (1897). It wasn't until 1903, however, that the brand reached the summit of popularity when it was bought by Fernandez Rodriguez, nicknamed Pepin, one of the most remarkable figures in the history of the Havana. A Spaniard who emigrated to Cuba, Fernandez Rodriguez began his career as a director at Cabanas, one of the great brand names of the period on a par with Villar y Villar and La Corona. Pepin was obliged to resign his post at Cabanas when the company was bought out by American Tobacco. He immediately acquired Romeo y Julieta and set about building it into a major enterprise. He used methods that were entirely original for the times, such as the introduction of bonuses for employees to increase productivity. The result was a huge increase in the quality and volume of production. The company already employed one thousand four hundred *tabaqueros* at the time when Fernandez Rodriquez decided to move the business to Calle O'Reilly,

where it remains today under the post-revolutionary name of Briones Montoto. Naturally, the quality of the cigars was not left behind in the move. Different full-bodied models make up the brand such as the Salomones, the Coronación and the Romeo Grandes, all top-of-the-line cigars. Fernandez Rodriguez also introduced the use of personalized bands for certain select members of his clientele. Over twenty thousand different bands were eventually printed. In keeping with the eccentricities of his appearance, Pepin proved to be a master of publicity. A great fan of horse racing, he bought a thoroughbred and named the horse "Julieta," which he ran in all of the most important races throughout Europe. He also opened a cigar concession in the hotel Capulet in Verona—on the very spot where Shakespeare set the story of Romeo and Juliet. Until 1939, the concession offered a free cigar to every tourist who came to see the site where the drama of those two unhappy lovers took place. This legendary personality died in 1954 having made his mark permanently on the Havana. Today, even after the revolution, Romeo y Julieta remains a quality-crafted cigar, especially in the domain of the large full-bodied cigar models. The 1960's saw the introduction of the famous Cazadores (gran corona), the most formidable of the Havanas. Only a few of the models of Bolivar and Ramon Allones can compare for the remarkable quality of this cigar. If the series proposes an especial at 9 1/4 inches in length (the Fabulosos) it is above all in the churchill format that the brand excels, furnishing three notable models: the Churchills, the Clemenceaus and the Prince of Wales. It is to Romeo y Julieta that is owed the invention of this celebrated model, the churchill, intended as an homage to Winston Churchill, who was a great help in popularizing the model.

The tender tale of **Romeo and Juliet** *should not mislead one about the rough nature of these cigars, among the strongest of the Havanas.*

Churchills

If the majority of the cigar bands of this brand are red, the bands on the Churchills are gold. This sign of distinction goes with its popularity, but it's not to be confused with two other churchills by the same brand: the Clemenceaus and the Prince of Wales. Sold in aluminum tubes, which may be a handicap as far as humidification goes, this is a fairly full-bodied cigar with a lot of character and a harmonious aspect highlighting its excellent construction. If the excellence of a number of different Romeo y Julieta formats should incline us to present a more modest format, such as a corona or even a small corona, the well-justified reputation of this cigar obliges us to make special mention of it. An impressive cigar and an experience not to be missed. It is perfect after a good meal or on any occasion.

7 inches

47 ring gauge

Saint Luis Rey

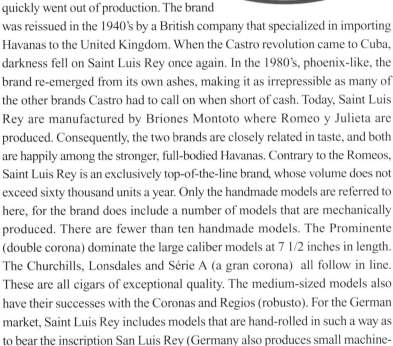

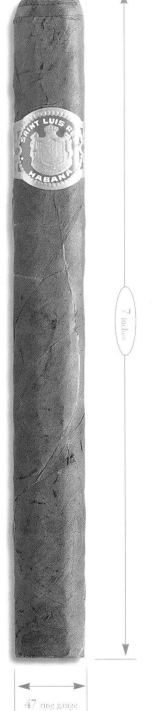

T he brand name Saint Luis Rey was registered in the nineteenth century by the company Zamora y Guerra. In spite of its great success, it quickly went out of production. The brand was reissued in the 1940's by a British company that specialized in importing Havanas to the United Kingdom. When the Castro revolution came to Cuba, darkness fell on Saint Luis Rey once again. In the 1980's, phoenix-like, the brand re-emerged from its own ashes, making it as irrepressible as many of the other brands Castro had to call on when short of cash. Today, Saint Luis Rey are manufactured by Briones Montoto where Romeo y Julieta are produced. Consequently, the two brands are closely related in taste, and both are happily among the stronger, full-bodied Havanas. Contrary to the Romeos, Saint Luis Rey is an exclusively top-of-the-line brand, whose volume does not exceed sixty thousand units a year. Only the handmade models are referred to here, for the brand does include a number of models that are mechanically produced. There are fewer than ten handmade models. The Prominente (double corona) dominate the large caliber models at 7 1/2 inches in length. The Churchills, Lonsdales and Série A (a gran corona) all follow in line. These are all cigars of exceptional quality. The medium-sized models also have their successes with the Coronas and Regios (robusto). For the German market, Saint Luis Rey includes models that are hand-rolled in such a way as to bear the inscription San Luis Rey (Germany also produces small machine-made cigars that sell under this brand name).

Churchills

The selection of formats offered by this brand is relatively narrow, if the machine-made formats are excluded. However, what is on offer is more than adequate and serves in some sense to herald the return of Saint Luis Rey to its former place among the elite brands. Presented here is the Churchill. More than the Prominente (double corona) or The Regios (robust), we have preferred to present the Churchills, which together with the Hoyo de Monterrey, is the sweetest among other Havanas of the same formats. There is a honeyed undertone that complements very nicely the full-bodied flavor of these cigars. A fine smoke after lunch, but it may catch the uninitiated off guard. To be smoked leisurely.

7 inches

47 ring gauge

Sancho Panza

The brand Sancho Panza was first registered in 1848 by Emilio Ohmstedt, a German-born merchant who was also owner of El Rey del Mundo. His small factory on the Calle de los Angeles was no match for the large industrialized establishments of the day, the two most formidable being H. Upmann and Partagas. Ohmstedt's cigars were therefore successful among a primarily local clientele. Hardly King of the World, and more of a Don Quixote, Emilio chose the name Sancho Panza for his other brand because the name of his alter ego had already been snapped up as a brand name. So Sancho Panza and his prudent pragmatism would have to do. After his death in 1870, the brand was bought by Salvador Paret, owner of El Colosos de Rodos, among other brands. But the success of these cigars remained on the local level until business began to decline at the end of the century, forcing Paret to close up shop the very year of Cuban independence, 1898. In 1904, the brand was picked up by the firm Munoz, Alonso y Cia. It was then that the brand made its great success on the international market with two legendary models, the Molinos and the Sanchos. Their popularity, however, was not enough to sustain Munoz, Alonso y Cia, and the company went out of business in the 1920's. The destiny of the brand after that was uncertain and erratic. It was to pass through the hands of a number of different Houses, such as that of Ramon Allones and H. Upmann, before this prodigal brand returned home to El Rey del Mundo. Today, the Sancho is manufactured by Briones Montoto (ex-Romeo y Julieta).

These cigars are easy to smoke, being ideal for the as-yet uninitiated because of their smooth, unctuous aroma. The line is restricted with only nine models on offer, but all are hand-rolled and of excellent construction. The great classics such as the Molinos (lonsdale) and the Sanchos (an especial 9 1/4 inches long) are still worth every minute of the two hours it takes to smoke one. The Dorados is another excellent lonsdale and worthy of its predecessor. The brand has a number of other attractive models to propose, like the Coronas Gigantes (a light churchill that is surprising given the format's reputation for heaviness). There are also the Coronas and the Torquitos (both coronas) and two petits coronas, the Bachilleres and the Non Plus. The Belicosos, a cigar with a pointed butt, weighs in at 5 1/2 inches with a diameter of over 4/5 inches (the largest of the line), and is a cigar that is far from being bellicose, despite its name.

It should be noted that a brand called Sancho Panza used to be manufactured in Mexico, and may be back on the market in the near future. The commercial rights to the brand belong to Villazon and Co., also owners of El Rey del Mundo, which are made in Honduras. Those who prefer the heavier-bodied Havana may find fault with the unusual lightness of the Sancho, but it nevertheless remains one of the best introductions to the Havana that can be found today on the market. Perhaps because Don Quixote is a national hero in Spain, Sancho Panza is one of the most popular brands of Havanas in that country.

The Sancho Panza for its subtlety at the summit of the mild Havana. Hard to do better: the legendary Sanchos and Molinos are superbly mild. The Belicosos (left), which are among the best torpedos in the world, are appreciated for their mildness and lightness.

Sanchos

**This is an especial, a top
of the line cigar and
a product that is sure
to keep the faith among
the more demanding
customers of this brand,
especially those who are
able and willing to pay
the price, for this large cigar
is one of the most expensive.
At 9 1/4 inches long,
a Sanchos can take up to
two hours to smoke, but
every minute is to be
savored. Indeed,
it is a smoke in three acts:
the first act is full of aroma
and sensation; the aroma
increases during the second
act, reaching a crescendo,
followed by an agreeable
and satisfying denouement.
This cigar is known for
its mildness, and its docile—
even vegetal—smoothness
and does honor to the
duration, if not the "power,"
of the experience.**

9 1/4 inches

47 ring gauge

Dominican Republic

Through such brands as León Jimenes, Juan Clemente, Davidoff, Arturo Fuente, The Griffin's, Santa Damiana and Ashton (opposite page), the Dominican Republic has, in a few short decades, become the "other" cigar country, surpassing even Cuba in exports. For centuries, the island of Hispaniola, currently divided between Haiti and the Dominican Republic, was little more than a dot on the map of the Caribbean (below), a representation of the Americas as known by Spanish navigators in 1647), and remained in the shadow of Cuba as far as the production of tobacco and cigars was concerned.

In 1994, the Dominican Republic became the largest worldwide exporter of hand-rolled cigars: ninety million units against Cuba's fifty-five million. This figure is phenomenal when one considers that exports were zero at the beginning of the 1960's. Arguably a disaster for his own country's cash flow, Castro was the best thing that happened to the Dominican economy. Castro, of course, would be the first to point out that, despite the boon to the economy, things haven't changed much for the average Dominican. Whatever the case may be, Cuba has lost its supremacy in the manufacturing of fine cigars, and the world no longer lives by the slogan: "If it's not a Havana, it's not a cigar."

Prior to the 1959 revolution, the Dominican Republic was something of the poor man of the tobacco trade. The dark tobacco it produced was considered too mild and lacking aroma. Consequently, there was no demand for

Dominican cigars on the international market. Nevertheless, the country provides excellent conditions for growing tobacco. It is located on the other side of the Caribbean, some five hundred miles from Cuba, but it has almost the same climate and soil as Cuba—the exceptional conditions needed for growing tobacco. It also has a similar cultural heritage dating from before the time of Columbus, who, of course, was the first European to arrive on its shores in the year 1492. The native Arawak Indians, like their cousins the Tainos, had been cultivating and smoking tobacco for centuries. Spain, the colonial overlord until 1844, had little interest in the Dominican leaves, and concentrated its efforts on developing the tobacco trade in Cuba.

In fact, Dominican tobacco received scant attention until the beginning of this century, when Cuban seeds were first imported. Plantations multiplied over the island, but the tobacco was essentially for export to manufacturers in Europe and the United States, where it was used for making second-rate machine-rolled cigars. Then came the revolution. The result was that a whole generation of Cuban emigres set up home in the Dominican Republic, among them tobacco specialists who began cultivating different varieties more suitable to the new environment. Naturally, they used Cuban seeds. It was after the 1962 embargo that the bonanza occurred, but not to the extent that had been expected. The United States consumed eighty-five percent of the Cuban production of tobacco, but instead of turning to the Dominican Republic for its supplies, the American tobacco merchants went shopping elsewhere in the tropical tobacco belt.

In response, the Dominican government created the "Dominican Republic Institute of Tobacco," an institute devoted solely to agricultural research in tobacco. Also, the infrastructure of the island's tobacco trade was revamped, with the consequence that laborers and peasants were

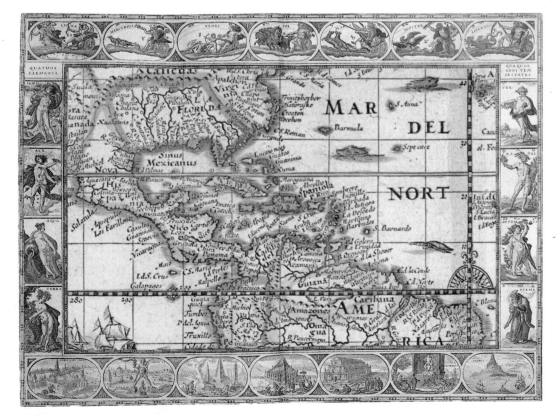

Davidoff

Aniversario
Nº1

Chateau Fuente

HAND MADE   HAND MADE

25 León Jimen

SANTA DAMIANA

LA ROMANA

Santa Da
Church
La Romana, Domini

THE GRIFFIN'S

Classic

Hemingwa

JUAN CLEM
churchill

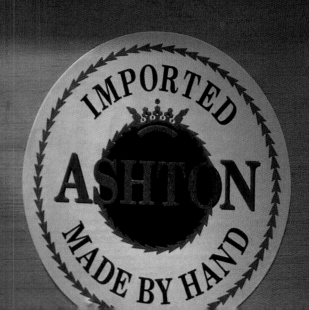

IMPORTED
ASHTON
MADE BY HAND

recruited for work on the new plantations. However, the enormous investment was hampered by political instability and an ongoing guerrilla war that kept investors at bay. In 1969, the tobacco colossus, Consolidated Cigars, made a timid attempt to test the waters when it transferred production of their brand Primo del Rey to the island. Another bold pioneer was Manufactures de Tabacos S.A. (Matasa), who in 1972, transferred production of Juan Sosa from Miami to the Dominican Republic. But even then, production didn't get fully under way until 1978, when the Sandinistas overthrew Somoza in Nicaragua. Suddenly, with neighboring Honduras under threat from the Red menace, the Dominican Republic began to look like just about the best place in the tobacco belt for growing the precious plant. Given the sudden change in conditions for growing tobacco in Nicaragua and Honduras, all that was left to do was to take the field, and the tobacco manufacturers finally sat up and took notice.

In 1979, General Cigar established a factory in Santiago in the northwest of the country. Soon the factory was producing a few of the the company's best brands: Partagas, Ramon Allones, Canaria d'Oro. Not to be outdone, Consolidated Cigar dove right in, setting up a factory in La Romana on the island's southern coast. This gigantic plant was to employ some one thousand six hundred and fifty individuals. Since 1982, all of its brands have been transferred to the Dominican Republic: Montecruz (of Montecristo fame), H. Upmann, Don Diego... Having blazed the trail, other companies soon followed. From Florida, the Fuentes arrived and, in a few years, they would become the largest producers in the country, with more than twenty-five million units now produced each year from four different manufacturers. Clearly, this country offers the best conditions both for growing tobacco and for making a fortune. The tobacco is inexpensive, the labor cheap and plentiful and the local authorities friendly, even granting the companies tax free status provided their products are not sold on the local market. Fair is fair.

In 1990 came the stunning transfer of Davidoff, which made the move to Santiago in order to develop a new and lighter line of cigars. And so a nobody, an underdog in the tobacco world went on to defeat the reigning and uncontested champ. Cuban hegemony had been eclipsed; it marked the

Stripping is an essential operation in the preparation of cigar wrappers. This process consists in removing the central vein of the leaf and its ribs by tearing them out between the thumb and index finger. Each half leaf so obtained is used for the wrapper (the binders on the other hand are made up of two half leaves). The stripping is traditionally the work of women, the despalilladoras, who perform the task with the help of a wooden board placed on their laps.

Harvest scene in the tobacco-rich valley of Yaqui, in the northwest of the country (here on one of the plantations owned by Tabacos Dominicanos, the manufacturer of Davidoff). The Yaqui Valley, from the name of the river which passes through it, is the second-largest tobacco-growing region in the world for high-quality cigars— after the Vuelta Abajo in Cuba.

Two separate fermentations over a three-month period of time are required for the tobacco to lose its natural acidity, which is due to the resin contained in the leaves. The leaves are sorted and brought to the "fermentation house," where they are stacked in a rigourously controlled environment with temperatures below 65°F. For the better brands, a third fermentation takes place, this time at the factory. It can last anywhere from one to four years.

end of an era. Nevertheless, this success has, in part, its origins elsewhere. Just as Castro had banned the Havana shortly after the revolution, the American people, led by the surgeon general and a battery of lawyers, have made significant headway towards prohibiting the cigarette. Their success was such that by 1993 a power vacuum had emerged and cigar sales skyrocketed. A new and burgeoning clientele appeared and their demand doubled exports in a few short years.

Before 1993, exports stood at some fifty-five million units; today it is over one hundred million units, making the Dominican Republic the largest exporter in the world, far ahead of Honduras, Jamaica and Mexico. Europe, traditionally its second-largest client, consumes barely a third of the Dominican production, and so it seems the Havana still has

an ally in the Old World. Today, the Dominican allure remains irresistible. Dozens of new brands, mostly American in origin, are created there each year, and there seems to be no end in sight. We might even expect the Marlboro Man, currently being driven into exile on his Camel, Joe, to kick the habit, get with the program and come in for the big win in the Dominican Republic. In 1996, the government of the Dominican Republic reserved more than eighteen thousand acres of land just for growing dark tobacco. That is twice the amount of land used for tobacco in the preceding years. The plantations are located in the northwest of the country, in the Yaqui Valley. The Yaqui Valley is the Dominican equivalent of the Vuelta Abajo, and the second-largest production zone in the world of high-quality tobacco. As in Cuba, the land is divided into *vegas,* the most renowned of which are Villa Gonzales, La Canela and Jacagua. Three types of tobacco are grown for cigars there. A local variety called *olor dominicano* is used to make the mildest models. Two Cuban varieties, *piloto cubano* and *San Vincente* are also used for the more full-bodied models. The *piloto cubano* comes from seeds from the Vuelta Abajo and is by far the richest and most aromatic of the three varieties. The *San Vincente* is a hybrid derived from the *piloto cubano.* About four thousand five hundred growers work the Yaqui Valley. On the best lands, fewer than three acres are actually exploited. Nevertheless, it is done at a handsome profit. Since the watershed year of 1993, the price of tobacco has risen remarkably, with increases of up to sometimes seventy-five percent from year to year. The harvest is usually purchased by middlemen, who in turn sell it off to the manufacturers. Some growers, however, are bound by contract to particular manufacturers.

For example, Tabacos Dominicanos (Davidoff) maintains in the Villa Gonzales area an exclusive network of some forty plantations in addition to its own. The largest manufacturers are established in the heart of the Yaqui Valley in Santiago and Villa Gonzales. It is not unusual for one of these factories to employ several hundred rollers, for the volume of production coming from these manufacturers is on the order of several million units a year. The Fuentes for example require some five hundred rollers to meet the demand. Some of the larger brand names are manufactured in the company's own factories. Others rely on locally owned factories with solid reputations. The company selling the brand Paul Garmirian for example has its hub in Washington yet entrusts the manufacturing of its cigars to Tabadom (Davidoff). Even though the Dominicans don't have the long tradition of manufacturing hand-rolled cigars that the Cubans have, they have more than proven their dexterity in the construction of the different models. It takes six months to properly train a roller, but at the end of that period, he is earning every penny he makes. The demand for good rollers, following the proliferation of new factories, has meant that a roller's average salary has soared to more than fifteen times what it was before 1993: one dollar a day. In thirty years of manufacturing, Dominican cigars have only gotten better, and their current reputation is rightly

earned. Indeed, not only has the Dominican Republic pummeled Cuba in the arena of the international market, it has also achieved the seemingly impossible: a fair comparison to its adversary in terms of quality. The problem of the tobacco's strength and aromatic qualities nevertheless remains. For that reason, the tobacco is usually mixed with other varieties and used as filler, and less often, as the binder. Consequently, stronger tobaccos need to be imported, generally from Honduras, Mexico and Brazil. Another weak point is that the Dominican leaves are unsuitable as top-quality wrappers. These also need to be imported, principally from Connecticut (Davidoff), Cameroon (Partagas) and Ecuador (Sosa). All the same, the Fuente family did succeed recently in producing authentic Dominican wrappers, derived from *piloto cubano* leaves. These are, of course, the superb rose-tinted leaves used in making the line Fuente Fuente Opus X.

To roll a cigar by hand is no easy matter: the filler is first molded in the palm of the hand, rolled in the binder and then in the wrapper. Then the "head" is shaped either into a round, flat or pointed end. The "foot" is then cut using the "calippers" (above left) and the "guillotine" (above right) to assure that the cigar has the right size down to the inch. Although the tradition of the roller is not as old as it is in Cuba, the Dominican rollers (below) have acquired in the last few years a reputation equal to their counterparts in Havana.

Arturo Fuente

Tabacalera A. Fuente y Cia is today the largest manufacturer of hand-made cigars in the Dominican Republic and, consequently, one of the largest in the world. The company produced more than twenty-five million cigars in 1995, with the Arturo Fuente models accounting for half of that figure. The remaining fifty percent are divided up among different auxiliary brand names, properly belonging to the company or franchised out to other manufacturers such as Montesino, Ashton, Cuesta-Rey, Bauza and Diamond Crown. The Fuentes, an old Cuban family, have been involved in cigar manufacturing since the last century. At the beginning of the 1900's, Arturo Fuente, the patriarch who would later give his name to the brand, decided to leave the island to give it a shot in the United States. He settled in Tampa, Florida, where in 1912 he opened a small business. The buildings were destroyed in a fire in the middle of the 1920's. The Fuentes were obliged to start from scratch, with a lapse of twenty years before they were able to return to the manufacturing of cigars. It was under Carlos Fuente, the grandson of Arturo, that the business would grow in size. At the beginning of the 1980's he decided to leave Tampa for the Dominican Republic, where his hand-rolled cigars are currently made. Financial success was easily won with the arrival of a new prosperity in 1993. Today, the family has four manufacturers in Santiago, with five hundred rollers just for the creation of the Arturos. There are some twenty different models making up the Arturos, which are known for their very aromatic yet light flavors. The tobacco filling and inner wrappers are a blend of Dominican leaves. The wrappers themselves mostly come from Cameroon—with the exceptions of Chateau Fuente, Double Chateau Fuente and the Royal Salute, which are rolled in Connecticut leaves. The series has recently

been expanded with the addition of the Hemingways (the Masterpiece, the Classic and the Signature) and the Don Carlos with three different models of limited production (only one hundred thousand units). This exclusive brand is made of tobacco harvested and fermented over at least ten years. In 1992, Carlos Fuente and his son, now director of the company, involved themselves in a risky gamble that most would have considered foolish if not ill informed. They decided to prove it was possible to cultivate Dominican leaves that could be used as cigar wrappers. Until that time, the unsatisfying quality of the Dominican leaf made it useful only as a filler and binder. After huge investments made at El Caribe, their tobacco farm, they went on to develop a new tobacco variety with *piloto cubano,* which yields superb red wrappers. These wrappers are good enough to compare with those from Cameroon and Connecticut. They have been employed since 1995 as the wrappers of a new line: Fuente Fuente Opus X. Seven models have already been produced with an annual production in the order of one million units. The Double Corona or the Perfecxion #2 are considerably more expensive than the Arturos. But the price must be paid for every innovation that leads to an improvement, for the quality of these cigars is irreproachable.

The Fuentes, an old Cuban family now living in the Dominican Republic, offer very aromatic light cigars, the most exemplary of which are the Hemingway series and the Opus X.

Opus X No. 2

*The line of formats offered
by Arturo Fuente has grown
spectacularly over the past
few years. The Hemingway
series and Opus X have most
recently been added.
Some of the formats have,
however, become difficult
to find on the market—
indicating that demand
has outstripped the supply.
The attention to quality,
notably in the time
expended on fermenting
the leaves, continues to
distinguish this brand from
the lesser Havana and
Dominican brands.
Recently, Opus X has been
the star of the line.
Its foremost member,
Torpedo No. 2, is a serious
rival to Montecristo No. 2
and figures as a symbol
of the line's success. Arturo
Fuente is the first brand
name to manufacture cigars
entirely from Dominican
tobacco—including the
wrappers, which normally,
for other cigars of this
equatorial region,
come from Cameroon or
Connecticut. The Dominican
wrapper used here is indeed
excellent, having a dark
color and oily texture,
the flavors being perfectly
matched to their wrappers.*

6 1/4 inches

52 ring gauge

Ashton

The brand name Ashton belongs to an American company from Philadelphia. Its hand-rolled models are nevertheless manufactured by the Fuente family (Tabacalera A. Fuente y Cia.) at Santiago in the Dominican Republic. The Fuentes also manufacture a number of brands for other companies. That makes for a yearly production of a few tens of millions of cigars in addition to their own brands. A few examples are Cuesta-Rey and La Unica, which belong to the Newman family of Tampa, Florida. Since 1986, the Fuentes manufacture the Newman's handmade models in exchange for which the Newmans continue production of a number of Fuente's machine-made brands in Tampa. The Ashtons are excellent cigars with a somewhat rich but light taste. They are made of Dominican tobacco for the filling and the underwrappers while the external wrappers are from Connecticut. The line includes around twenty models found in a number of diverse formats: from the Cabinet No. 1, a 9-inch-long giant (nevertheless, very light) to the elegant Cordial at 5 inches. In addition to the standard series, which includes, among others, the Churchill, the Prime Minister and the Magnum, are the Ashton Cabinet Selection series, the lightest of the line, and the Ashton Aged Maduro series, made with dark (maduro) wrappers from Connecticut. The Ashtons are primarily sold on the American market, but have found a sizeable opening on the British market as well, where the name Ashton comes from—in honor, ironically, of a famous English pipe manufacturer.

6 1/2 inches

44 ring gauge

8-9-8

The brand offers a rich line of formats as varied as the most extensive Havana brands. These cigars are of an excellent and elegant construction, and certain formats have dark brown maduro wrappers as preferred by a sector of the clientele. Compared to its homologue from Partagas, the Ashton 8-9-8 is less blunt and more refined, while at the same time being more aromatic and lighter.

Avo

Who would have remembered Avo Uvezian, the forgotten composor of the immortal *Strangers in the Night,* if he hadn't been the namesake of one of the finest cigars of the Caribbean? What is an Avo but a luxurious blend of sensuous rhythms and blue curls of voluptuous smoke? If that sounds a bit too much, it wasn't enough for Avo Uvezian, a man who put his whole soul into the art of good living, investing his energies wisely in the writing of hit singles and the production of fine cigars. Avo was born in Beirut. At the end of the 1940's, he began a career as a pianist in a jazz trio destined to be a brilliant success throughout the Middle East. So spectacular was his success that he became the Shah of Iran's personal piano player. However, Avo was not satisfied jazzing it up for a King of Kings, and decided to chance it among the glitter of the United States, where he composed tunes for the music producers and radio stations. If music be the food of love, Avo quickly recognized that man cannot live by love alone. He lit upon the cigar as a way to expand his financial horizons and undertook the creation of his own brand, which he chose to establish in the Dominican Republic. The brand is associated today with the Davidoff group, which manufactures the cigars in Villa Gonzales (at Tabadom) to the beat of three million units a year. The cigar filling and the inner wrappers are Dominican while the wrappers come from Connecticut. The series, registered among the lighter cigars, includes some fifteen different models. The standard series includes the Avo No. 1 to 9, the Belicoso, the Little Belicoso and the Pyramid. In 1996, the Avo XO series appeared. There are three models in the series each named after a musical movement, connecting once again the voluptuous blue curls to the sensuous rhythms of Avo's first love, music. They are the Preludio, for that morning smoke, the Intermezzo for the lunch break and the Maestoso for the grand finale of the evening out.

Belicoso

Very pleasant, somewhat full-bodied, this excellent cigar is part of a family that offers three other quality models, the Pyramid of a superior size and diameter, the little Beliscos, just as wide but of a smaller length, and the XO series, the Intermezzo, also of the same diameter, but of an intermediate size. If the Intermezzo is notable for its spicy and ample flavor, the Belicoso remains the closest to the recognized qualities of the Avo, qualities that can be described as vegetal, herbal and even heavy with an excellent, regular combustion.

6 inches

44 ring gauge

Davidoff

"Smoke less but better: make of it a ritual, a philosophy." Wise words indeed, as we would expect from Zino Davidoff, the most famous cigar merchant in the world. Davidoff died in Geneva on the 14th of January 1994, at the age of 88. His life story is inseparable from the history of the Havana, and he is perhaps the one figure most responsible for promoting the Havana as an essential article of good living. Zino was born in the Ukraine in 1906. He was the son of a tobacco blender who went into exile in 1911 to escape the anti-Semitic pogroms raging across the land. His father made his way to Geneva with the family in tow where he opened a small shop specializing in tobacco from the Orient. One of their most notable clients, an avid consumer of cigars, was a Russian outlaw by the name of V. I. Lenin, also a notorious welcher who left behind a large unpaid bill when he trotted off to free the masses. Zino himself was destined to assume control of the family business and soon an empire was built. Between 1924 and 1929, much in the spirit of Peter the Great, he undertook an extended tour of tobacco plantations across Argentina, Brazil and Cuba in order to study the production cycle. Enlightened by these first hand experiences, he returned to Geneva and installed Europe's first humidified cigar cabinet. The tobacco store soon became one of the "in" places among the Old Continent's havanophiles. With the arrival of the war, Davidoff astutely cultivated his connections in Cuba. He gained control over large stocks of cigars destined for Europe, those that remained blocked by the war in warehouses, and he personally took responsibility for emptying the stocks at a sizeable profit. It was in 1946 that inspiration struck, appropriately while he was perusing a wine list at an exclusive restaurant. The bright idea was to refashion the image of the Havana after that of the great vintage wines. This innovation revolutionized the marketing of cigars, introducing for the first time the concept of the "luxury cigar." The complex elaboration of this concept closely followed the lines used to promote the finest wines, and within a year, the concept passed into

practice with the introduction of the legendary Châteaux series: Château Margaux, Lafitte, Haut Brion, Latour and Mouton-Rothschild, respectively. The cigars were manufactured by Hoyo de Monterrey from the finest tobacco blends from the Vuelta Abajo. They were to become, along with the Montecristo, the best cigars of their day, and were to play a key role in the reintroduction of the Havana to Europe in the immediate post-war period. Zino was again a central figure in the history of the Havana when, in the early 1960's, he almost single-handedly saved it from the legacy of Lenin by aiding the Cubans in re-establishing the product on the international market. In return, the Cubans allowed Davidoff to create his own brand, which was named appropriately after himself. The first models appeared in 1969 with the No. 1, the No. 2 and the Ambassadrice. The Châteaux series were soon included in the line, along with the newly created Dom Perignon and the "Mille" series. The year 1970 marked a turning point, when Zino, feeling the effects of age, passed on the torch to a new generation. His group was integrated into Oettinger Imex, a tobacco importer located in Basel since 1875, which was under the direction of Ernest Schneider. Thus, the Schneider era succeeded the Davidoff era. This period was to see profound changes in the commercial strategy of the group. Schneider went on to develop a vast network of outlets for the sales of Davidoff, involving subsidiaries, boutiques, distributors, sales agents and, where the whole story began, exclusive restaurants. The group currently has holdings in over sixty countries. More than forty different stores are under the Davidoff name in Europe, in United States (New York, Beverly Hills) and Asia, where a Davidoff store stands proudly in the heart of Beijing. In 1985, the group

Zino Davidoff (1906-1994) was in his day the "Pope of the Havana." Since 1990, the Davidoff are manufactured in the Dominican Republic, and the quality, like the name, endures.

began a frenzied period of activity diversifying at an astonishing rate. There are now Davidoff sunglasses, Davidoff leather goods, Davidoff T-shirts, Davidoff cognac, Davidoff vodka and Davidoff perfume... With revenues totaling $450 million, the group has more than succeeded in realizing its dream of conquering new frontiers, for sixty percent of that figure has only a remote connection with cigar sales. Indeed, even the fate of the cigars would blow with the prevailing winds. In 1990, after consulting with Zino himself, Schneider decided to stop the Cuban production of the cigars and transferred the operation lock, stock and barrel to the Dominican Republic. This shrewd move was motivated in part by an ambition to capture the market for light cigars, then experiencing a tremendous wave of popularity. This required the introduction of a new generation of Davidoff targeted for the American market, which was inaccessible from Cuba due to the embargo. Interestingly, this gambit had been tried before in 1977 with the creation of the Zino in Honduras. The rupture with Cuba was final, and there have been no Davidoff Havanas available since 1993, much to the chagrin of the regular Davidoff consumers. Nevertheless, the group still imports 2.5 million Cuban cigars each year to stock its boutiques. The first Dominican Davidoff models appeared in 1991. They are manufactured by Tabacos Dominicanos (Tabadom), which is overseen by Hendrick Kelner. They also produce for Davidoff other brands such as The Griffin's, Private Stock and Avo. The volume of Davidoff production stood at six million units in 1996, a quarter of which is destined for the United States, their largest clientele. The meticulous care taken in the manufacturing of these cigars remains the Davidoff hallmark. The filling is made from a blend of no than four Dominican tobaccos, with an exceptional period of fermentation lasting up to four years. The line includes around twenty different models which according to their lightness is divided into five different series. The lightest are the Davidoff series: No. 1, 2 and 3, the Tubos and the Ambassadrice, and the Aniversario series (No. 1 and No. 2). Slightly more full-bodied cigars make up the Mille series (Davidoff 1,000 to 5,000) and the Grand Cru (No. 1 to 5). The strongest cigars are in the Special series (Special T, R, C, and Double R). The Special C, it should be noted, is a culebras—three cigars woven together, a format that only Partagas and H. Upmann in Cuba manufacture today. As quality (and luxury) oblige, the Davidoff are among the most expensive cigars available.

Davidoff benefit from an aging process that lasts four years for each of the four varieties of leaf used in the filler. That explains the remarkable success of such models as the Grand Cru and the Special.

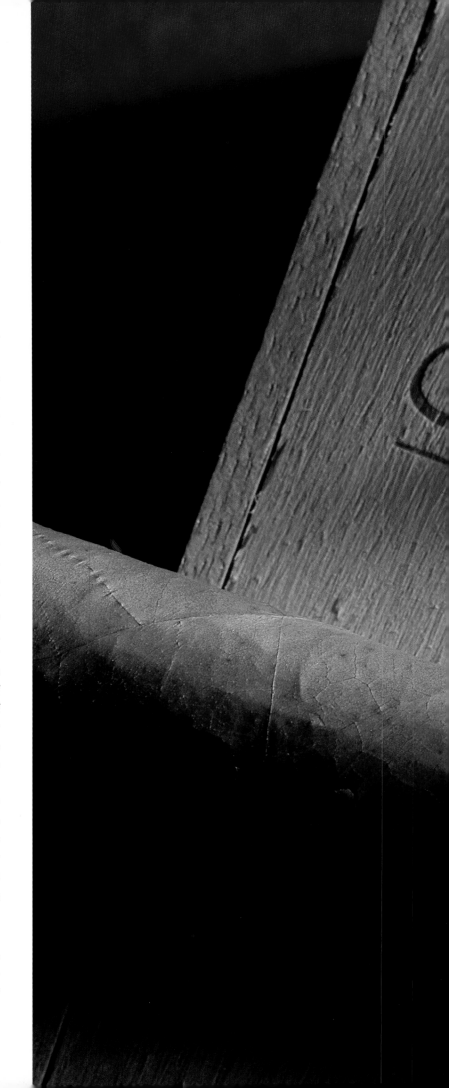

Double R

**This double corona
embodies the great
tradition of Davidoff.
It is the best representative
of the art and culture
of the cigar. It has all the
makings of a great classic:
a distinguished shape and
a generous, pronounced
aroma that lasts throughout
the whole smoking
experience. This cigar is the
product of a complex and
subtle blend of four different
tobaccos from four different
harvests. It is a justified
member of the Special
series, alongside Davidoff
Special R, Davidoff Special T
and Davidoff Special C.**

7 1/2 inches

50 ring gauge

Hecho a mano
República Dominican

Davidoff
Double «R»

Hecho a mano
República Dominicana

25 Davidoff

Double «R»

Davidoff

Davidoff
Double «R»

Davidoff
Double «R»

La Gloria Cubana

E l Credito Cigar Co. began production of La Gloria Cubana in Miami in 1972. It is owned by Ernesto Perez-Carillo, a Cuban who spent most of his career as a tobacco exporter. Elected to the Senate in 1954 as a representative of the province of Pinar del Rio, he was forced into exile in 1959 as a result of his connections with the Liberal Party. During that time, he acquired the commercial rights to the historical brand La Gloria Cubana, which followed him into exile in Miami's Little Havana. In 1968, he opened a small manufacturing company and released his first American brand: El Rico Habano. Then La Gloria Cubana in 1972. After the death of Ernesto Carillo in 1980, El Credito's production would fall to five hundred thousand units per year. Not until the turning point of 1993 did production in Miami bounce back with Ernesto's son at the helm. Supported by some thirty

rollers, production is now at full capacity with 1.2 million cigars rolled each year. That made way for the introduction of two new brands: La Hoja Selecta and Dos Gonzales. But La Gloria Cubana remains the standard bearer, accounting for almost nine hundred and fifty thousand of the

cigars made today. Miami does not have an abundance of good rollers, so in 1995, El Credito opened a new manufacturing plant at Villa Gonzales in the Dominican Republic. Production at Villa Gonzales runs to some six million cigars a year, of which 3.5 million are La Gloria Cubana. The same tobacco is used for the Miami and Dominican Glorias; the filling is Dominican and Nicaraguan. The inner wrappers are Nicaraguan and the superb exterior wrappers are from Ecuador. The Gloria are strong cigars, certainly the cigar closest to the original Cuban flavor. The series offers five different models with emphasis on the larger cigar: the Soberano, the Charlemagne, the Churchill, the Torpedo (a piramide) and the Wavell.

Soberano

This brand is one of the most popular in the world, especially in the United States, where it benefits from the aura surrounding its Cuban homonym. The quality of the wide variety of formats is indisputable, and the taste and aroma testify to the brand's well-deserved reputation. The Soberano is one of the most impressive cigars in our selection. It is a sort of super double corona, larger and longer than the Double Corona from La Gloria Cubana. In terms of size, it comes right after the Crown Imperial, which heads the list.

8 inches

52 ring gauge

The Griffin's

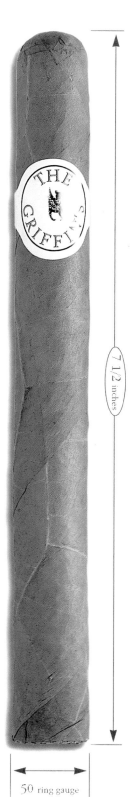

7 1/2 inches

50 ring gauge

The brand The Griffin's, introduced at the beginning of the 1980's by Bernard Grobet, belongs today to the Oettinger-Davidoff group. The different models are manufactured in the heart of the tobacco-rich Yaqui Valley by Hendrik Kelner, director of the manufacturer Tabacos Dominicanos (Tabadom). A native to the island, Hendrick Kelner is one of the most sought-after experts on the Dominican cigar. He started Tabadom in 1984, first to produce The Griffin's and later, at the beginning of the 1990's, to produce the other Davidoff brands (Davidoff, Avo, Private Stock). Davidoff and Tabadom are today involved in a joint venture. Tabadom also manufactures the brands of other companies such as Paul Garmirian, Troya, Montero and Match Play. That makes for a production volume of about fifteen million units each year, all from the hands of only one hundred and twenty rollers. The Griffin's account for about 1.2 million cigars manufactured by Tabadom in 1996, but is expected to account for up to three million in 1997. The Griffin's are made from a blend of Dominican tobaccos for the filler and the binder, while the light-colored wrapper comes from Connecticut. The line includes a dozen or so models, with a spread of different, very satisfying formats, from the Don Bernardo at 9 inches long to the Griffinos at 3 3/4 inches, one of the smallest cigars currently available on the market. A supplementary tip: The Griffin's are a good buy as far as quality is concerned.

Prestige

This is an excellently crafted cigar and characteristic of the best cigars from the Dominican Republic. It is an elegant churchill and comes second in size among the other formats which are offered by the brand. The brand is connected with the Davidoff works, which helps to assure its quality. This is an everyday cigar, light and mild, even a little sweet, with a discreet aroma that makes it easy to smoke.

Juan Clemente

No relation to Roberto. The brand Juan Clemente was launched in 1982 by a Frenchman, Jean Clément, who hispanicized his name in order to add a little local color to his cigars. He is not the only Frenchman operating in the Dominican Republic. Bernard Grobet, who created The Griffin's, is another Gallic compatriot. The French have a long history in the cigar trade. Tobacco was introduced to the French in the sixteenth century by Jean Nicot, whose name is more familiar to botanists as the namesake of *Nicotiana tabacum* and to consumers as the plant's highly addictive endogenous chemical—nicotine. The French have cultivated a dark variant of tobacco on their native soil with which they have been making cigars since 1740. The manufacturing of cigars in France is controlled by the powerful State tobacco company, the Seita, which produces about two billion units a year (though ninety-five percent are in fact cigarillos). That makes the Seita the second-largest manufacturer in the world, after the American company Consolidated Cigar. In the Dominican Republic, the brand Pleiades is manufactured for the Seita, with some two hundred thousand units imported each year. Nonetheless, the Dominican models are not as prized in France as their Cuban counterparts which have an import volume of six million units yearly. The Juan Clemente are made of Dominican filler and binder wrapper and rolled in Connecticut wrappers. The line offers a dozen different formats: from the Especiales at 7 1/2 inches long to the Demi Corona at 4 inches.

6 7/8 inches

Churchill

This churchill is the best of the brand and easy to recognize: the band is on the other end of the cigar. Plain yet light and somewhat spicy, this Juan Clemente is a good place to start for the uninitiated, even if the format, like the three other large cigars of the line, seems better suited to the more experienced smoker.

JUAN CLEMENTE

46 ring gauge

GARANTI
CIGA
TOTAL
A MANO C
DE T
SEL

ZAMOS QUE ESTOS
ROS HAN SIDO
MENTE HECHOS
ON HOJAS ENTERAS
ABACOS PUROS
CCIONADOS

0166578

HINE

CIGAR RESERV
COGNAC

24 JUAN CLEMENTE
churchills

JUAN
CLEMENT

E. León

HECHOS A MANO
REPUBLICA DOMINICAN

León Jime

SELECCION ESPECIAL DE TABACOS

León Jimenes

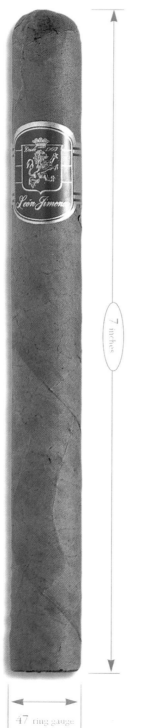

For many years, the brand name León Jimenes has gotten the vote from cigar lovers everywhere. The brand's line of light, aromatic and creamy cigars has earned it a place among the most distinguished brands from the Caribbean. The subtle blend of Dominican tobaccos *(Olor dominicano,* essentially) that go into the different formats testifies to an unusual amount of cigar making know-how. Indeed, the Jimenes family has been manufacturing cigars since 1903, which makes them the oldest cigar manufacturers in the country. That date is scrupulously noted on the cigar band as if to set the brand apart from most other Dominican brands which have appeared on the market only recently. The cigars are hand-rolled by the manufacturer La Aurora, which also produces excellent cigars of the same name. The principal difference between La Aurora and León Jimenes is in the respective wrappers: while León Jimenes are rolled in Connecticut wrappers, La Aurora are rolled in wrappers from Cameroon and are considerably spicier. The line is somewhat modest in the number of models offered. Only thirteen different models are registered in the catalogue. The numbered models 1 to 5 offer a series of formats declining in size with each respective number, from the impressive No. 1 at 7 1/2 inches X 50 ring gauge to the elegant No. 5 at 5 inches X 38. All the same, it is in the non-numbered models that the cigars with the largest diameters are found, with the Torpedo at 58 ring gauge, the Petit Belicoso at 52. The latter formats are just as satisfying and light as the numbered formats, a sign perhaps that girth is no obstacle to subtlety.

No. 2

A churchill made of a mix of tobaccos noted for their pronounced flavors; it is without doubt the outstanding cigar of the brand. Part of a series of a dozen or so formats, this is a pleasing robusto and an excellent Figurado Belicoso. Each of the León Jimenes is identifiable by its bronze-colored wrapper of Connecticut leaves. It smokes nicely with its spicy accent and touch of sweetness.

Partagas

Partagas is, along with Macanudo, one of the most popular brand names sold by General Cigar. More than eight million Partagas cigars are produced every year—still more than half as much as Macanudo. This prestigious Cuban brand name (begun in 1845) was bought by the American company in 1975. Its owner at the time was Ramon Cifuentes, whose family had controlled Partagas since 1900. Exiled from Cuba after the revolution, Ramon Cifuentes abandoned all hope of ever recovering possession of his business in Havana. The factory in Cuba still produces Partagas but under the manufacturing name of Francisco Perez German. Partagas is one of six original Cuban brand names which General Cigar possesses the rights to sell on the American market. The others are: Ramon Allones, Cifuentes, Cohiba, La Flor de Cano and Bolivar. The last two have still to be commercialized. The Dominican Partagas are full-bodied cigars, rolled in beautiful dark wrappers from Cameroon. The filler is

Mexican and Dominican in origin and the binders are Mexican. Recently added to the standard series (which includes, among others, the Partagas No. 10, the Aristocrat and the Purito) are the Partagas Limited Reserve, cigars of limited production as the name indicates, with only fifty thousand produced during the best years. The Royale, the Regale, the Robusto and the Epicure are unimpeachable models, except for maybe the price: you'll have to lay down a bit more for them in comparison to the Partagas. In homage to Ramon Cifuentes, General Cigar recently launched a new brand named Cifuentes by Partagas, which is manufactured in Jamaica.

Humitube

*Tradition and finesse are the hallmarks of this cigar.
If the legacy of the Havana of the same name has not been
entirely preserved by the Dominicans, this line of some ten
different formats is not lacking in character. The filler
is made from a mix of Mexican and Dominican tobaccos.
The binder is Mexican and the wrapper is from Cameroon.
These cigars have an earthy, woody flavor that is not as
pronounced as the Havana of the same name. This lonsdale
benefits from the preservative properties of the tube
in which it is sold. It is one of the smoothest and subtlest
of cigars on the market.*

6 3/4 inches

43 ring gauge

Honduras

Don Lino, Puros Indios, Punch... Honduran cigars are notable for their smooth and mild characteristics (opposite). They have won a reputation for quality in the last several years and are now very competitive with the Dominican products. The country is today the world's third-largest exporter of hand-rolled cigars.

An integral part of the great Mayan empire, the people of Honduras began cultivating and smoking tobacco very early on. Discovered in 1502 by the Spanish (below: an old map of Central America), the country would not gain an international reputation until 1962, when it took advantage of the embargo of Cuba by the United States.

The country of Honduras extends over a major portion of the lands of the ancient Mayan civilization. The Lencas of today, like the Chortis, are the direct descendants of the Indian populations that originally cultivated tobacco in the Copán Valley. It was colonized by the Spanish from 1523 to 1821, though the land was only sparsely used for the cultivation of tobacco (the leaves being considered too mild for smoking). Nevertheless, a rich cigar tradition was to develop here. A perfect example is the small manufacturer in Santa Rosa de Copán that is still active today since its founding in 1785, a date that precedes the first manufacturers in North America. The Honduran product, however, would remain confined to the local market over the next few centuries. It wasn't until the Cuban revolution in 1959 that foreign investors began to take interest in Honduran tobacco. Honduras benefited from a number of anti-Castro exiles who would go on to boost the cigar trade there by cultivating new varieties of toabacco from Cuban seeds. Among the more famous tobacco barons to set up shop in Honduras is Fernando Palicio, who would relaunch the production of Belinda in 1962. He was associated with two tobacco merchants who had been in the Honduran trade since the 1950's: Dan Blumenthal and Frank Llaneza. The latter would eventually buy Belinda and other Palicio brands such as Punch and Hoyo de Monterrey. They are today, under the name of Villazon & Co., among the largest Honduran manufacturers, with thirty-five million hand-rolled cigars made each year. In the early 1970's, Honduran production stood at twelve million cigars a year with only four manufacturers rolling for the international market. Interest in Honduras was only slight. In 1972, the American group United States Tobacco International began production in the country, conferring upon Central American Cigar Inc. (CACSA) the manufacturing of its brands Astral and Don Tomás. In 1977, Davidoff opened a factory in the Copán Valley for the production of its first non-Cuban brand—the Zino. Honduran tobacco suffered a setback with the outbreak of the Sandinista revolution in neighboring Nicaragua.

The troubles would continue until 1990 with frequent guerrilla incursions that involved burning and raiding the tobacco plantations and cigar factories. With the war in Nicaragua, a number of growers fled to Honduras, where they reinvigorated the Honduran trade. That was the case with Nestor Plasencia, a Cuban who first fled to Nicaragua in 1965, and who was obliged to flee again in 1979. Starting from zero in Honduras, he began by buying up plantations before manufacturing his own cigars in 1985. His reputation is such that a number of foreign companies have called on him to act as a consultant. Today, Nestor Plasencia is responsible for the production of some thirty different brands of international standing (V Centennial, La Mocha, Don Juan, La May) with no fewer than

four different manufacturers in his possession. Honduran cigars have recently acquired a reputation for excellence that has put them in close competition with Dominican products. The different formats are very light, rich in aroma— and the Hoyo de Monterrey Excalibur, made by Villazon, are now considered the best non-Cuban cigars in the world. The noted quality of Honduran cigars explains how the country has gone on to become the third-largest exporter of hand-rolled cigars in the world, after the Dominican Republic and Cuba. Its largest client is the United States, which consumed sixty million units in 1996. The best cigar tobacco is grown in the Jalapa Valley, in the southwest of the country, on the border with Nicaragua. The plantations are centered around the cities of Danlí, Moroceli and Talanga. In the latter town, UST owns more than one thousand three hundred acres of tobacco-growing land, which makes it one of the largest landowners in Honduras. Contrary to that of the Dominican Republic, the soil of Honduras is perfect for

growing superb dark wrappers, which come from Connecticut seeds. The leaves from which the filler and the binder are derived are grown from Cuban seeds. To bolster the aroma, the filler is generally mixed with tobacco imported from the Dominican Republic, Ecuador and Costa Rica.

The principal manufacturers are set up in Danlí, which is somewhat like Villa Gonzales in the Dominican Republic. There are a dozen factories in the town which produce fifty million cigars annually, a figure that accounts for nearly half of the Honduran export volume. The most noted specialists in the country are Raymond F. Guys (Central American Cigars Inc.), Nestor Plasencia (Fabrica De Tabacos Oriente) and Rolando Reyes (Cuba Aliados Cigars).

The volume of production from each manufacturer is on the order of several million units, with nine million produced by Central American Cigar Inc. alone. In more human terms, that translates into about five hundred hand-rolled cigars per day per individual roller.

Don Lino

The brand Don Lino first saw the light of day in 1989 in Honduras. At that time, the explosive prosperity enjoyed by cigar manufacturers had not yet reached the country, and exports of cigars to the United States stood at no more than twenty-nine million units. Today, exports to the United States have soared to well over sixty million units a year. Don Lino has proven to be most adept at profiting from the surge in cigar sales that began in 1993. Witness the astounding succession of new models added to the line each year, with more than twenty-eight models currently held in Don Lino's stable. Despite this proliferation, the brand maintains a standard of excellence with a variety of flavors, ranging from very light to medium full-bodied cigars. The filling and the inner wrappers are made exclusively of Honduran tobaccos, all grown from Cuban seeds. The wrappers are from Connecticut and are more or less light-colored, depending upon the series. The standard series includes some fifteen different models ranging from the impressive Supremos at 8 1/2 inches in length to the delicate Epicures at 4 1/2 inches. Some models are demurely numbered from 1 to 5, a practice that has been a tradition of the trade since the time of the celebrated Montecristo of 1935 (and, like many traditions, has little if any intrinsic sense to it). Next in the line are the Habana Reserve series: eight excellent models (notably the Churchills, the Tubo and the Toros), all having benefited from an aging process lasting four years. Finally, there is the Colorado series whose four models are readily identifiable by their dark wrappers. They are the Presidentes, the Torpedos, the Lonsdales and the Robustos.

Churchills

A well-named series that is the top of the line offered by this recent brand. The brand also offers a variety of fine formats as well as the notable Colorado series of the rich, dark wrappers. Light- to medium-bodied, this churchill best incarnates the other side of the Honduran cigar: a lot of aroma without being too assertive, a fine burning quality characteristic of the majority of products from the same area, and a few heavy accents which, son the contrary, are lightly spicy.

7 1/2 inches

50 ring gauge

MADE IN HONDURAS

Havana Reserve

DON

Havana Reserve

By

FINEST HAND MADE
DON TOMÁS
LONG FILLER CIGARS
GRAN FABRICA
DE TABACOS
RIZED TOBACCO GROWN FROM HAVANA SEED
EDITION

Don Tomás

United States Tobacco International is a powerful American consortium specializing in light tobacco (Copenhagen) and wine (Château St Michelle). In Honduras, the group also has a thriving trade in hand-rolled cigars. Among their brands figures Astral, their main brand, and Don Tomás. UST International has its plantations in Talanga, not far from the capital, Tegucigalpa. The varieties of tobacco cultivated in Talanga are from Cuban seeds and account for the filling and inner wrapper. The leaves for the wrappers are also cultivated in Honduras, grown from Connecticut seeds. The harvest is dried on the premises and then shipped to the manufacturer in Danlí. The manufacturer is Central American Cigars S.A. (CACSA), directed by Raymond Guys, one of the foremost specialists on the Honduran cigar and a resident since 1972. With some fifteen hundred employees, CACSA has a production volume on the order of nine million units a year. The brand Astral accounts for over one million of that figure, followed by Don Tomás and a number of other brands. The Don Tomás is a fine cigar with a blunt, full-bodied flavor—much more full-bodied than the average Honduran cigar, though not nearly as much as the Cuban. The line, divided into three series, offers about a dozen models which, for the most part, are large caliber cigars such as the Gigante (8 1/2 inches long), the Imperial (8 inches) and the President (7 1/2 inches).

Special Edition

This family of cigars is composed of three complementary series: Don Tomás Special and Don Tomás International are perfect examples of the success that the Honduran cigar currently enjoys. Mildly full-bodied to heavy, Don Tomás No. 300 Special is notable for its mollifying qualities, its easy-to-smoke character and its rich flavor. It is agreeable to every kind of smoker, from the beginner to the most experienced.

Excalibur

oyo de Monterrey Excalibur is considered by many to be the best cigar in the world, and—havanophiles would hasten to add—the best non-Cuban cigar in the world. They are made in Honduras by Villazon, who acquired the commercial rights in 1965. The different formats, rolled in superb Connecticut wrappers, are remarkably mild and even smoother than the standard Hoyo de Monterrey. The series is limited, offering only seven different numbered models in a variety of satisfying formats from the No. 1 at 7 1/4 inches long to the No. 7 at 5 inches. It should be noted that the cigars are known as Hoyo de Monterrey Excalibur in the United States, while in Europe they are known simply as Excalibur, a difference with no bearing on their quality. The cigar bands proudly bear the name of José Gener, founder of the historic Hoyo de Monterrey (1867). José Gener was also a celebrated brand name from Havana, to which Villazon acquired the rights for

the American market the same year that Hoyo de Monterrey came under its dominion. Villazon is today one of the largest owners of the

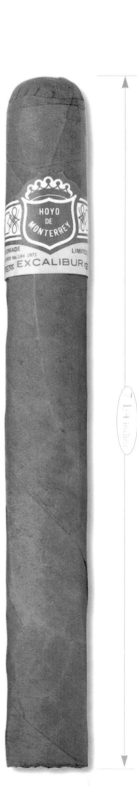

historic brand names, alongside Consolidated Cigar, owners of Montecristo, H. Upmann, Por Larrañaga, La Corona Cabanas, Henry Clay and Santa Damiana. Also in the running is General Cigar, the owner of Partagas, Cohiba, Ramon Allones, Bolivar, Cifuentes and La Flor de Cano. This situation is temporary since it is likely that Villazon will be bought out by General Cigar.

No. 1

This large churchill, rolled in Honduras, continues the great tradition of Hoyo de Monterrey. It has an excellent flavor and a magnificent construction. This cigar also has an imposing presence due to its large diameter, the largest in our selection. Mildly full-bodied, with an earthy, somewhat green accent, it is easy to smoke, like most of the other formats in the series, which includes another notable cigar—the Bouquet, a churchill closer to the specifications of the format. There is also the No. 2 of the same size, but with a slightly smaller diameter.

Punch

Punch is a very old brand from Havana, first introduced there in 1840. Since 1965, the company Villazon & Co. (owned by Dan Blumenthal and Frank Llaneza) has held the commercial rights for the American market. The rights were acquired from Fernando Palicio, the last Cuban owner of the brand, who like so many others was chased into exile when the Red tide rolled into town. He was also the owner of Belinda, Hoyo de Monterrey and of José Gener, which also would fall into the hands of Villazon. Villazon is solidly ensconced in Honduras with an annual production of hand-rolled cigars in the order of thirty-five million units. Like all of the cigars produced by Villazon, Punch are fairly full-bodied models. The filler is made from a Dominican, Honduran and Nicaraguan blend while the binder is Ecuadoran. The line offers about twenty different models, with

an emphasis on the larger calibers, such as the Presidente at 8 1/2 inches, or the Diademas and the Gran Diademas at 7 1/8 inches each (but with a diameter exceeding 4/5 inches). Also note the impressive 7-inch Casa Grande. On the coronas formats, excellent models like the Super Selection No. 2. Next comes the Delux series: the Superiores Delux and the Britania Delux, followed by the Grand Cru series: Château Lafitte, Château Corona and Château Margaux (barely disguised rehashes of the lauded Château Davidoff). These last are by far the richest cigars of the line—and a lot less expensive than their homonyms.

Monarcas

**The saga of Punch continues beyond the shores of Cuba with this impressive churchill, which like its Cuban counterpart, is packaged in an aluminum tube.
It is a well-crafted cigar and burns nicely like the other Honduran Punch, all the fruit of a selective blend of Honduran, Nicaraguan and Dominican tobaccos. This cigar has an Ecuadoran wrapper. Full bodied, with a spicy, peppery accent, the flavor of the cigar is sensitive to the means by which it is stored. The aluminum tube in which it is packaged is an undeniable advantage, provided the cigar is smoked while it is still fresh and properly humidified.**

6 3/4 inches

48 ring gauge

Puros Indios

Puros Indios is made by the company Cuba Aliados Cigars. It was started by Rolando Reyes, one of the last originals from the pre-Castro era of the Havana. Born in Cuba three-quarters of a century ago, Reyes entered the cigar business at the age of fourteen. He would be apprenticed in some of the largest and best workshops in the industry: H. Upmann, Partagas and Romeo y Julieta. By 1955, Reyes had learned enough to start up his own brand, Cuba Aliados. It was an immediate success.

Four years later, with the arrival of the 1959 revolution, the products of Rolando Reyes, which had expanded with the addition of several newer brands, reached the comfortable level of over six million units annually. All the same, the new regime, however impressed, was not pleased. All of the brands were confiscated by the government, and in 1970, Rolando Reyes had no other option but to go into exile. He set up in Miami, where, after working several odd jobs, he resumed production of hand-rolled cigars. In 1990, Reyes decided to move production to Danlí in Honduras. Here, his cigars quickly earned the reputation of being most like the Cuban originals.

The business, which is now run by Rolando's son, currently boasts a production volume of five million cigars a year, with Puros Indios accounting for over one million. Aliados, the first historical brand introduced by Rolando Reyes, is still in production.

6 1 2 inches

46 ring gauge

Piramides No. 1

Even if this is a recent brand, developed after the embargo of Cuba, it has nevertheless benefited from the old traditions that have created the best Honduran cigars. Full of flavor with remarkable sweet and earthy overtones, this cigar is also notable for its fine burning qualities. The Piramides No. 2 also deserves special attention due to its rich and varied flavor. The No. 2, though slightly smaller and less thick than the No. 1, must also be included in any selection of excellent cigars.

Zino

In 1977, Davidoff pioneered his first non-Cuban cigar when he acquired tobacco plantations in Honduras. The word "pioneer" is indeed the appropriate term since Honduran cigars at the time were virtually unknown on the international market. Once again, the purpose of this venture was to try and sidestep the American embargo of Cuba. Capital being mobile despite political intransigence, this was the first step that Davidoff was to take in abandoning Cuba in favor of the Dominican Republic. In Honduras, the Swiss consortium opted to set up shop in the Copán Valley, a rich tobacco-growing region that had long been exploited by the Mayan Indians. The manufacturing plant was dubbed La Flor de Copán, and their product, the Zino, is made of Honduran tobacco for both the filler and the inner wrapper, while the exterior wrapper come from Ecuador. The utmost care is taken in producing the various models, which are particularly rich in aroma and remarkably mild in taste. The line offers approximately twenty-five models. The standard series combines the qualities of mildness and lightness throughout the nine different models, which offer the best choice of formats: from the Zino Princesse at 4 inches in length to the Zino Veritas, which is 7 inches. The Zino Tubos No. 1 comes in an aluminum tube, as the name indicates. In 1987, the Connoisseurs was introduced, a new series launched in honor of the opening of Davidoff's first boutique in New York: the three models numbered from 1000 to 3000 are characterized by their heady aroma and their exceptional lightness.

Next, there is the Zino Mouton Cadet series, the most prestigious of the line. Much like the Châteaux series of the magnificent Cuban era of Davidoff, the Zino Mouton Cadet takes its cue from the label of one of France's most cherished wines. They are specially selected for the Baroness Philippine de Rothschild, the proprietor of the Bordeaux *grand cru,* and thus offer cigar lovers a blend of two great traditions in excellence. The Zino Mouton Cadet include four models numbered from 1 to 4, in a highly accommodating array of formats: from the No. 1, which is 6 1/4 inches in length, to the No. 4, which is 5 inches long. The wrappers for these cigars are top of the line, and have been fermented for over a five-year period. The Zino Light Line, as the name suggests, are especially light cigars that are made from Brazilian and Sumatran tobacco. This series includes the Zino Classic and the Zino Relax and is intended for the occasional smoker or for the debutant. Also under the brand name Zino are European-manufactured cigars that are noted for their "Dutch flavor": the Zino Drie and the Zino Jong, which essentially are made from Indonesian tobacco. Zino makes two other little "Specialties," both from Brazilian tobacco: the Zino Santos and the Zino Por Favor.

Zino is historically the first non-Cuban brand of the Davidoff-Oettinger group and predates the Dominican Davidoff. The brand has widespread appeal due to its top of the line products, such as the Zino Veritas and the Zino Mouton-Cadet.

~ 114 ~

Zino Veritas

Zino

ND MADE
ONDURAS

Mouton Cadet No. 6

The Honduran brand Zino by Davidoff is in a league of its own, yet still embodies quality and care that distinguishes the great Swiss name. Aromatically rich, yet smooth, the Mouton Cadet No. 6 has a loyal following among connoisseurs who appreciate its flawless construction and its creaminess. Occasional smokers will enjoy the lightness that makes it one of the most accessible cigars in our selection.

Jamaica

The island of Yamayca, as it once was called by the Arawak Indians because of its fertile soil (bottom, an old representation of the island), is today the fourth-largest exporter of

hand-rolled cigars in the world. The mildness of these cigars makes them a serious rival to the products of the Dominican Republic and Honduras.

Jamaica was discovered by Christopher Columbus in 1494. The island was then populated by the Arawak Indians, who called the island Yamayca, meaning "fertile land." Its tropical climate and well-irrigated soil were ideal for the cultivation of tobacco. Like the Arawaks throughout the West Indies, they smoked tobacco in pipes or rolled in leaves. The English took over from the Spanish after 1655. The island came under dominion of the Crown, and it soon became the most important colony of the region. The English established plantations and factories, principally around the capital, Kingston. Many of the original brands are still sold today, such as Macanudo (1868), Temple Hall (1876) and Royal Jamaica (1922). Jamaican cigars, as part of the Commonwealth, were largely intended for the British market; and though they can hardly rival their Cuban counterparts, they are a good deal less expensive due to the heavy taxes levied on Cuban imports. After the country's independence in 1962, the year of the embargo of Cuba, the United States began to take notice of the Jamaican goods. Because of their mildness, they enjoy a reputation among American consumers equal to that of the Honduran products. The General Cigar Co. soon established a formidable presence in Jamaica after it bought Macanudo, its widest-selling brand, and Temple Hall. Its rival, Consolidated Cigar, has less of a presence on the island. Nevertheless, it has owned Royal Jamaica, the island's foremost brand, since 1988. That year, a hurricane slammed into the island, completely destroying the factory in Kingston. The owners at that time, Robert and Philip Gore, had no recourse but to sell the brand to Consolidated Cigar (the producers of, among others, Montecruz and H. Upmann). The new American owners immediately undertook the transfer of production to the Dominican Republic, building a new factory at La Romana—where they had earlier established a large cigar factory at the

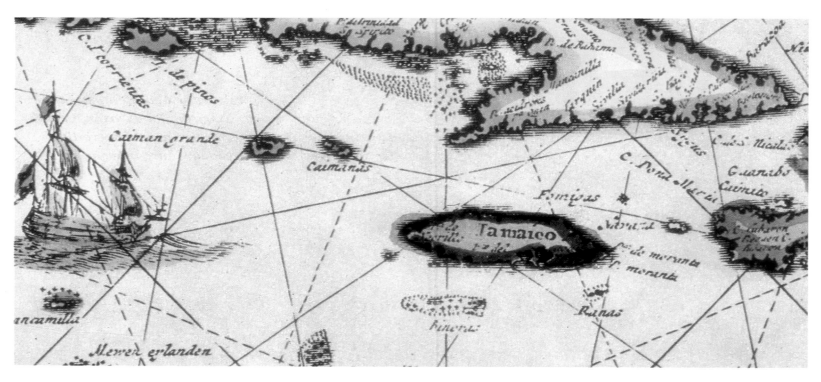

beginning of the 1980's. Some one hundred rollers are employed there yielding an annual production of 3.5 million cigars. Then, in 1996, Consolidated Cigar transferred production back to Jamaica at Maypen near Kingston. One might speculate that the move was prompted by a desire to recapture the British market, since the British had stopped importing Royal Jamaica after the island's independence from Britain. That accounts for a loss of revenue on some five hundred thousand cigars a year. The decision to resettle near Kingston could only please the Jamaican government, who saw Royal Jamaica as part of the national patrimony and, need it be said, a non-negligible source of income and employment. A

free trade status, unfettered by taxes, was granted to the brand in gratitude for its return to the country. Jamaican tobacco is grown from Cuban seeds. The tobacco's mildness requires that it be mixed with tobacco from Honduras, Mexico and the Dominican Republic for the filler and binder. The wrappers themselves are imported from Connecticut, Brazil and Indonesia. Since 1993, Jamaica has significantly benefited from the American trend in smoking hand-rolled cigars, making Jamaica the third-largest exporter to the country, behind the Dominican Republic and Honduras. In 1995, fifteen million Jamaican cigars were sold in the United States, double the previous years.

Harvesting tobacco at a plantation near Kingston. Today, as in the past, mechanical means of harvesting tobacco leaves are inadequate. In fact, the three different types of leaves from the three different levels of the plant must be harvested according to the extent of their maturity. Each provides a different tobacco variety: the ligero *are the upper-most leaves on the plant, the* seco *are from the middle, and the* volado *come from the lower part of the plant.*

Macanudo

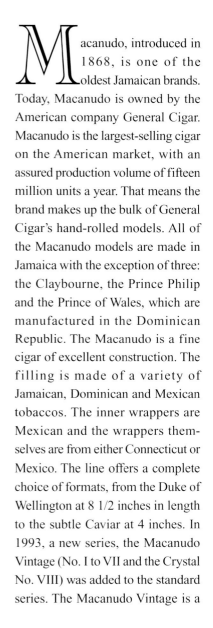

Macanudo, introduced in 1868, is one of the oldest Jamaican brands. Today, Macanudo is owned by the American company General Cigar. Macanudo is the largest-selling cigar on the American market, with an assured production volume of fifteen million units a year. That means the brand makes up the bulk of General Cigar's hand-rolled models. All of the Macanudo models are made in Jamaica with the exception of three: the Claybourne, the Prince Philip and the Prince of Wales, which are manufactured in the Dominican Republic. The Macanudo is a fine cigar of excellent construction. The filling is made of a variety of Jamaican, Dominican and Mexican tobaccos. The inner wrappers are Mexican and the wrappers themselves are from either Connecticut or Mexico. The line offers a complete choice of formats, from the Duke of Wellington at 8 1/2 inches in length to the subtle Caviar at 4 inches. In 1993, a new series, the Macanudo Vintage (No. I to VII and the Crystal No. VIII) was added to the standard series. The Macanudo Vintage is a favorite among cigar lovers who prefer the fuller-bodied models, but they are appreciably more expensive than the other Macanudos. A new clientele appeared in the United States when the cigar concept was relaunched in 1993. This considerably younger clientele developed its own habits of consumption, which General Cigar tapped into by opening its Club Macanudo in New York in 1996. The "cigar bar" was born, offering a place of refuge where smokers can relax over a drink with their favorite brand and puff away without incurring the wrath of the neighbors. Today, there are five such examples of this phenomenon in New York, and these trendy establishments are favorite resorts among the young who are determined that youth shall not be wasted on them. These establishments offer in fact a convivial and benign way of outraging the equally trendy anti-smoking morality that has swept across the nation.

7 1/2 inches

49 ring gauge

Vintage 1993 No. 1

Macanudo Vintage, not to be confused with the Macanudo Regular from the Dominican Republic, are simply the best of Jamaican cigars. They are prized for their rich, ample aroma, and the tobacco is aged four years. The Macanudo Vintage 1993 No. 1 heads this excellent series. Not too light, not too strong, it is for the experienced smoker.

Nicaragua

Nicaragua, a country discovered by the Spanish in the sixteenth century (see map below), is today the emerging power in the production of hand-rolled cigars.

Nicaragua shares with Honduras a fertile area for growing tobacco. It is situated in the northwest of the country in the Jalapa Valley. The plantations are concentrated around the towns of Estelí and Ocotal, where they benefit from well-irrigated, sandy soil and a climate having a moderate humidity of about seventy percent. The tobacco plants are grown from Connecticut seeds for the wrappers and a variety of Cuban seeds for the filler and binders. Consequently, the Nicaraguan cigars are justifiably compared to those from Honduras. Foreign entrepreneurs have taken an interest in the country since the 1960's—the period during which Joya de Nicaragua became one of the most highly esteemed brands throughout Central America. In 1970, the Cuban Jose Padrón transferred his operations from Miami to Nicaragua, giving an enormous boost to the local industry. It was not to last, due to the outbreak of war in 1978, which would destabilize the country until 1990. The ruling Sandinistas were not keen on the idea of foreign merchants and industrialists operating on their soil; the plantations were torched and the factories demolished. Another round of exile had begun for Cuban growers such as Nestor Plasencia. He would flee into neighboring Honduras, where he soon established himself as the leading cigar producer in that country, with over thirty different brands entrusted to his care by different foreign companies (making for more than thirty million hand-rolled cigars each year). Bad luck only brings more bad luck, and at the beginning of the 1980's, the "blue mold" struck, spoiling the recent harvest and wiping out the rest of the crop. The "blue fungus" also devastated the other tobacco-producing countries throughout the Caribbean and Central America. In Cuba, where the debacle began, Castro even went as far as to accuse the United States of waging biological warfare against Cuba's socialist economy. Propaganda aside, the epidemic of blue fungus was stopped faster than the Contras could "democratically" oust Daniel Ortega in the 1990 elections, the same year that Joya de Nicaragua resurfaced on the international market. The country was left in ruins with a foreign debt of over $8 billion, but all signs indicate a quick recovery is underway. The large brand names are back in full production at the hands of manufacturers such as Tabacos Cubanica for Padrón and Tabacos Puros de Nicaragua for Thomas Hinds.

In 1992, Nestor Plasencia was offered four hundred acres by the Chamorro regime as compensation for his lost plantations. On that initiative, he has since returned to open a factory in Ocotal and, in 1995, another factory in Estelí. As the point man for Nicaragua's production of cigars, Plasencia and his factories are responsible for the manufacturing of some forty thousand cigars a day. Nicaragua is one of the least expensive countries in Central America, and that is its principal advantage. The low cost of production, including labor and materials, means that investors are likely to show more and more interest in the country, even more since the tradition of hand-rolling cigars is meticulously maintained by the Nicaraguan *torcedores,* in particular by the Indians.

By 1996, the country was already exporting ten million handmade cigars a year, which nearly puts it on a par with Mexico, yet still far behind the Dominican Republic and Honduras.

If Padrón is one of the oldest Nicaraguan brands, others such as José Martí and Segovia (above) are beginning to get their due on the international market. Grown from Cuban seeds, Nicaraguan tobacco closely resembles the tobacco of neighboring Honduras in the way of mildness and subtlety. Selling tobacco harvested in the Jalapa Valley (left).

Padrón

J ose Padrón was born in Cuba... literally into the tobacco trade. His family owned a number of lucrative plantations in the province of Pinar del Rio, and his grandfather was already busy at the turn of the century manufacturing cigars for the local market. When the momentous year of 1959 arrived, El Lider Massimo decreed the redistribution of land throughout the island, with the result that the Padrón family had their plantations confiscated. The only way out was exile. Jose fled with his family, first to Franco's Spain, where, upon second thought, he decided to move the wife and kids to Miami. There, in 1964, he opened a small factory in Little Havana, the traditional haven for Cuban refugees. The structure of the factory was completely simple: he was running the factory with the aid of one assistant. The cigars were made during the day and sold the same night in the local cafes and restaurants. In 1965, Padrón almost single-handedly produced sixty-six thousand cigars. That's the number reached today in a single week. In the meantime, the business has expanded. In 1970, Jose Padrón decided to leave Miami because of its lack of experienced rollers and transferred the business to Nicaragua. Today, he owns his own plantations there, as well as the manufacturer Tabacos Cubanica. In 1978, Padrón set up shop in Honduras, creating the manufacturer Tabacos Centroamericanos. All of the Padrón line, including the Honduran brands, are made entirely of Nicaraguan tobacco grown from Cuban seeds. The models are mild and of sturdy construction. To the standard line, which includes twelve different formats, has been added the Padrón 1964 Anniversary series: six formats of limited production that use only tobacco that has been fermented at least four years, which explains why the series is slightly more expensive than the preceding one.

5 inches

50 ring gauge

1964 Anniversary Series Exclusivo

A corona gorda, with the length of a corona but a much wider girth, this cigar is without question the best from Nicaragua currently available on the market. This is a cigar with character, made with exceptional care and enveloped in a beautiful dark wrapper.
It is a mollifying smoke, with an earthy yet somewhat spicy flavor and just a touch of sweetness. Perfect with a nightcap at the end of an evening.

Mexico

Nicotiana tabacum, the most widely consumed tobacco variety in the world, comes originally from Mexico, where it grew wild. It was first cultivated over three thousand years ago on the Yucatán peninsula, the cradle of the once-great Mayan civilization. To the Mayas, tobacco was a sacred plant given by the gods as a privileged means of communicating with them. Carvings have been discovered in Mexico depicting priests and gods smoking long rolls of tobacco while exhaling large clouds of smoke through the nose and mouth—what may be considered the oldest record of cigar smoking in the world. Tobacco was also used by the Mayas as medicine for the treatment of fever, rheumatism, snake bites and hunger. From Honduras, the cultivation of tobacco spread throughout Central America and eventually to North America via the Mississippi. The Spanish conquest in the sixteenth century brought to prominence the tobacco variety *Nicotiana tabacum,* which quickly supplanted *Nicotiana rustica* due to its richly aromatic qualities. Later, the variety was brought to Cuba, where it gave rise to the hybrid *havanensis*. In Brazil, another hybrid would emerge as *brasiliensis,* and North America would cultivate the hybrid *virginica,* while Southeast Asia cultivated *purpurea,* a direct derivative of *havenensis*. Modern Mexico, independent since 1821, developed its own

Mexican tobacco was initially valued in Europe for the ornamental characteristics of its beautiful flowers. It was then sought after for its medicinal properties, especially for the treatment of headaches.

Nicotiana tabacum *is indigenous to the Yucatán peninsula, where it grows wild. The Mayas began cultivating it and smoking it over three thousand years ago.*

tobacco industry early on. One of the largest tobacco producers in Mexico today is Jorge Ortiz Alvarez, owner of Tabacos Santa Clara and a direct descendant of one of Mexico's first tobacco-growing families. They first began production in 1830, a year honored by the brand name Santa Clara 1830. All the same, Mexican cigars would not enjoy an international reputation until 1962, the year of the embargo. The rift opened the way for such brands as Te-Amo, Costenos and La Prueba, which were quickly recognized by the American consumer for their outstanding quality. Today, Mexico is the fourth-largest exporter of hand-rolled cigars to America, with ten million units sold in 1995. The tobacco-growing area in Mexico is situated in the valley of San Andres in the state of Veracruz, where the Mayas themselves had originally cultivated tobacco. The main crop is reserved for the manufacturing of cigars, and a local variety, prized for its lightness, is mixed with a Sumatran variety to make the filler. This variety was introduced to Mexico in 1950 by Dutch growers who were then looking for new lands following the loss of their plantations in Indonesia.

They soon abandoned its cultivation in Mexico, but the Mexicans themselves continued to grow it. The Sumatran tobacco is currently one of the most common ingredients in Mexican cigars intended for export, and it is also responsible for the wonderful dark wrappers (maduro) which typify the Mexican products.

Consequently, Mexico does not need to import its wrappers, which make the cigars considerably cheaper than their competitors in Honduras or the Dominican Republic.

Available on the international market for only the last thirty years, the Mexican brands (above: Te-Amo, San Andres and Santa Clara 1830) benefit from a cigar tradition dating back two centuries (left: a Mexican factory at the beginning of the century).

A traditional puro is made by hand from the "head" to the "foot". The head is the butt of the cigar, while the foot is the end that is lit. Left: the finishing touches are put on the head, which can be round, flat or pointed.

Cruz Real

The brand Cruz Real was introduced in 1993. It was targeted at the American market as a rival to Te-Amo. This brand is not only the product of fine manufacturing, but also of an aggressive, take no prisoners marketing strategy. Consequently, it is one of the most visible brands in the United States. Cruz Real includes Costenos, La Prueba, Ornella and Santa Clara 1830. It has also a high profile in Europe, particularly in Switzerland and Italy, in addition to a growing presence in Canada. This fast food and soft drink homologue of the cigar industry is nevertheless a reputable hand-rolled cigar, manufactured by Tabacos y Puros in the rich valley of San Andres. The tobacco is pleasingly mild and the price is absolutely right for a cigar of this quality.

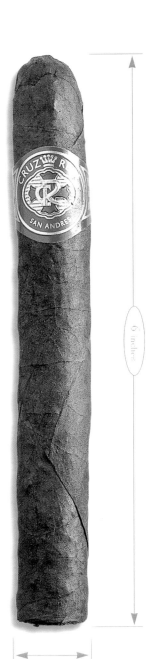

No. 19 Maduro

Te-Amo's main competitor among Mexican manufacturers, the brand Cruz Real has been for a long time a great source of promotion for tobacco from the San Andres Valley, one of the most reputable tobacco-growing regions in the world. The maduro wrappers are a specialty of San Andres. Cruz Real No. 19 is one of the best examples. The taste of this cigar is perfectly mated with its dark brown wrapper: it is fairly earthy, lightly spicy with a woody accent and more natural than refined.

Te-Amo

Te-Amo was launched in 1965 at the initiative of a New York financier. It was one of the first non-Cuban brands to appear on the American market. Its appearance was of course a direct attempt to capitalize on the embargo. Over the years, the Te-Amo have enjoyed significant popularity and are today, along with Macanudo and Partagas, the most widely sold hand-rolled cigars in the United States. The brand has been controlled by Consolidated Cigar since 1989. The different models are manufactured at San Andres Tuxtla in the state of Veracruz by the manufacturer Matacapan Tabacos, which is under the direction of Alberto Turrent Cano. Annual production stands at around eighteen million cigars, of which eight to nine million are Te-Amo. They also manufacture for Consolidated Cigar the brand Matacapan and, since 1996, the brand Excelsior. The Te-Amo are made only with Mexican tobacco grown and harvested in the San Andres Valley. Matacapan's plantations cover over one thousand acres of the valley. The dark wrappers (maduro) come from Sumatran plants, which were introduced in the 1950's by Dutch specialists. The line offers about twenty different models, ranging from mild- to medium-bodied cigars. It also offers the widest selection of different formats, from the C.E.O. at 8 1/2 inches to the Torito at 4 1/2 inches. The latter is a diminutive version of the famous Toro—6 inches long. But, however reduced in size, the girth of the Torito remains the same as the Toro. The Te-Amo, it should be pointed out, are among the least expensive of the large cigars.

6 inches

50 ring gauge

Toro

This corona gorda, with its rustic maduro wrapper, offers an unusual experience to smokers who are more familiar with Dominican and Honduran tobacco. This mild, somewhat full-bodied cigar is characterized by its unique flavor—an almost vegetal herbal-like taste. The cigar burns well, and all in all, typifies those qualities associated with tobacco products from San Andres, the region considered by Mexicans to be the best tobacco-growing land in the world.

Canary Islands

The discovery of the New World by Spanish explorers in the fifteenth century would result in one of the greatest "discoveries" of modern times: American tobacco. From 1520, the plant was cultivated in Spain. A century later, the cigar would be invented in the workshops of Seville Today, Spain is the last European country that maintains the tradition of hand-rolled cigars. These brands are excellent (shown here, the Condal), but nevertheless they have hardly any following on the international market due to the favor shown to Caribbean products.

Since the days of Antiquity, the pipe has been in use in Europe. Among other plants, the Greeks enjoyed smoking hemp, and the Celts were partial to wild lettuce for its mildly narcotic properties. But no plant in Europe resembled tobacco, the reason being that *Nicotiana* doesn't grow naturally in temperate regions. It wasn't until 1492, after the arrival of Columbus in America, that Europeans were first introduced to tobacco by the original cultivators: the Indians of the Caribbean. Tobacco was thereafter cultivated in Spain and Portugal. From there, cultivation spread north to France and England in the middle of the seventeenth century and east to Italy, the Balkans and finally the Ukraine and Russia. The plant was originally cultivated in Europe as an ornament. It then was discovered for its medicinal properties when ingested as a fine powder in the form of snuff to combat headaches. The first European smoker was a certain Rodrigo Jerez, a member of Columbus' 1492 expedition to the New World. He brought back bundles of tobacco to Barcelona and held the first public demonstration of how to consume it. Though the people were impressed, the authorities of the day took exception: Rodrigo was condemned by the Inquisition for the practice of witchcraft and spent seven years in prison as a result. Rodrigo's gift has not been forgotten, and today his name is honored by a yearly prize awarded in Cuba for the best book published on tobacco. Until the eighteenth century, the Spanish and the Portuguese were practically the only smokers of cigars in Europe. The word is thought to come from the Spanish *cigarra* meaning "cicada", presumably because of the similarity in form. More likely, it comes from the Mayan word *ciq,* meaning "to smoke". The first cigar factories appeared in Spain in the seventeenth century, but the real boom began in 1731 with the opening of the Royal cigar factories in Seville. They held a virtual monopoly on the manufacturing of cigars made from tobacco imported directly from Cuba. Their quality was such that they acquired the epithet "sevilla," after the same fashion as the "Havana."

In the nineteenth century, cigar smoking had reached its zenith, thanks largely to the armies of Napoleon, who had picked up the habit while waging war on the Iberian peninsula and ultimately on the rest of Europe. Suddenly, smoking cigars had become a sign of social distinction, an occupation of both the decadent bourgeoisie and the even more decadent artists of the times. Those were the days when someone like the great composer Franz Liszt, a newly converted religious mystic, would refuse to enter the monastery without some assurance that he could take a break between meditations and prayers to enjoy the transcendental pleasure of a fine Havana. Also at that time, the first female smokers appeared on the scene, luminaries such as Princess de Metternich and the writer Aurore Dupin, alias George Sand. Queen Victoria, on the other hand, saw things differently and would not tolerate anybody smoking in her presence, such was her Victorian horror of the cigar. At her death, her son King Edward VII would make up for lost time by becoming one of the most notable and compulsive cigar smokers in history. He was still to be outdone, however, by Winston Churchill, who, it is said, consumed the staggering amount of two hundred and fifty thousand in the course of his alloted time. The nineteenth century was also the period during which the Havana would cover Europe in smoke, eventually extinguishing the Spanish brands. Europe and the United States are currently the largest world-wide producers of cigars, although the majority of these products are cigarillos and rather mediocre machine-made models. Curiously, the largest tobacco consumers in Europe are not the Spanish despite their long history and crucial role in the dissemination of tobacco world wide. Rather, it is the Danish, followed by the Belgians, the Dutch and the Swiss, who are Europe's most avid consumers.

Of course, half of this consumption is in the form of cigarillos. Indeed, habits of consumption vary considerably in Europe from north to south. The Latin countries of France, Spain and Italy favor heavier-bodied, dark tobacco, which explains their enthusiasm for the Cuban *puro*. The northern countries, on the other hand, whether Scandinavian or Germanic, consume above all cigars characterized by the so-called "Dutch flavor," which comes principally from Asian-grown tobacco. This tobacco is significantly lighter-bodied and less aromatic than the Cuban varieties. The difference in a sense is historical in origin: South America was primarily in southern Europe's sphere of influence, while northern Europe preponderantly had its colonial interests in Asia. Most European states no longer cultivate their own tobacco, but prefer to import the leaves used in manufacturing their own tobacco products. There are, however, some notable exceptions, such as Greece, Italy, Spain and France. The latter is the largest European producer of cigars. A few of the available models, such as the Picaduros, are fabricated entirely from tobacco grown in the south of France, in the region of Bergerac. Italy grows its tobacco primarily in Tuscany and on the Pô plain. This tobacco is dark and very full bodied and is used in the famous Toscani brand of Italian cigars. Unfortunately, all of these cigars are machine made. Spain is in fact the last European

country where cigars are still hand-rolled. Such unjustifiably neglected brands as Calypso, El Guajiro and Don Julian are by far the best *puros* made in Europe.

Only those models made in the Canaries, however, have any international following as a result of competition from the all-powerful Havanas.

A tobacco plantation on the island of Lanzarote. The traditional weigh station between Spain and Latin America, the Canary Islands imported Cuban methods for cultivating tobacco and manufacturing cigars very early on.

Puros Vargas

Puros Vargas is perhaps the one brand most firmly established on the international market. Created by Enrique Vargas, the brand hails from Santa Cruz on the island of Palma. Santa Cruz was an ancient stopover for ships coming from the Americas. Consequently, tobacco was introduced early to the island. It was first cultivated there in the seventeenth century at the time when cigar technology was first exported to Spain from Cuba. By the nineteenth century, the reputation of the *cigarcanaria* (the cigar from the Canary Islands) was already well established through brands such as Don Alvaro de Torres Ruiz. After the 1959 revolution, many Cuban growers and manufacturers chose to continue their trade in exile in the Canaries, in particular, the brands Partagas (Cifuentes) and Montecruz (Menendez). These newcomers blew a breath of fresh air into the Canary trade, and were soon followed by other high-quality brands such as Dunhill. However, most of these brands, now in the hands of American owners, were transferred to the Dominican Republic during the 1980's. Local production is nevertheless a significant fraction of the market, manufacturing some four hundred million units annually, the vast majority of which are machine made. Three-fourths are exported to the United States and Europe.

If Puros Vargas takes the lion's share of the export volume, other brands have their fill as well, especially Casanova and Montecanario. The Vargas family alone manufactures 2.5 million units a year, including the brands Don Enrique, Pena, Tenegul, La Criolla and La Mia. The tobacco used in manufacturing these cigars is eclectic to say the least. It comes from Palma, Cuba, the Dominican Republic, Brazil and even Indonesia. These cosmopolitan blends are the hallmark of the Canary cigar and the open secret of its success.

7 1/2 inches

50 ring gauge

Churchill

Made in Spain, it is the best cigar coming from outside the Carribean and Central America. Ironically, the brand is hard to find in Spain, even though it has the official seal of the Royal Family. What could be better for the international market? Of a rustic appearance, with a beautiful brown wrapper, it has a wonderful finish to it, a somewhat earthy, slightly salty taste, which suffices for this churchill to be featured in our selection.

Philippines and Sumatra

In Asia, the opium pipe has long been the smoker's paradise. Tobacco, introduced in the seventeenth century by western merchants (shown above, a map of Asia at that time), nevertheless ended up replacing opium as the favorite smoke. Huge consumers of cigarettes, Asians never really took to the cigar—only Indonesia, Burma and the Philippines are an exception.

Among Asian countries, Burma is one that has developed a real passion for the cigar. Curiously, dark tobacco grown from Cuban seeds is traditionally rolled in plum leaves, and only the women smoke the larger formats.

Asia, contrary to Europe and the Americas, never developed a passion for cigars. This is the civilization of the pipe, which has been smoked here for over four thousand years. Pavot, from which opium is extracted, is what they traditionally smoked. Tobacco would sweep over Asia in the seventeenth century as a result of contact with European traders. The Chinese initially mixed it with opium to attenuate the narcotic effects of the plant, but by the nineteenth century, tobacco would completely replace opium. Plantations sprang up throughout China, and today the country is the second-largest tobacco grower in the world after the United States, but only for pipe and cigarette tobacco. Indonesia is one of the rare countries in the region where cigars are still hand-rolled, a tradition dating back to its days as a Dutch colony. Dark tobacco was introduced in the seventeenth century. It is mainly cultivated on the islands of Borneo, Sumatra and Java. The most aromatically rich local variety is *Nicotiana tabacum purpurea,* derived in the last century from Cuban seeds. The leaves make for excellent wrappers. Beginning in the late seventeenth century, the tobacco was exported to Holland, where the cigars were manufactured. This was the birth of the "Dutch flavor," known to be rather poor in aroma and considerably more acrid than the Caribbean *puros.* They nevertheless still have a loyal following, notably in northern Europe, where the tradition of the havana is less prevalent. Since 1949, independent Indonesia has been manufacturing its own version of the "Dutch flavor" cigars, but often the tobacco is blended with Brazilian varieties to enhance its aroma. All the same, it is in the export of wrappers that Indonesia has played an important role in the cigar industry. Their principal clients are the United States and Europe, which also use Indonesian tobacco in the fillers and binders. Burma, a former British colony, has itself cultivated a dark tobacco variety since the seventeenth century. It also is derived from Cuban seeds. Contrary to the rest of Asia, an authentic national cigar tradition persists in Burma. Here men, women and even children partake in its pleasures at any time of the day, though more often as an appetite suppressant. The cigars are of the homemade variety and, like their Indonesian counterparts, are distinguished by a rather pleasant acridness. It should be noted that the whitish wrappers come not from tobacco leaves, but from plum leaves. Interestingly, large formats are shunned by men, who fear that smoking them may attenuate their virility, and they are therefore reserved for a largely female clientele.

The Philippines, along with Indonesia and Burma, is Asia's largest producer of cigars. Tobacco was introduced to the islands in the sixteenth century by the Spanish conquistadors. Legend has it that it was Magellan himself who was responsible for its introduction when he left behind a few seeds from Brazil after discovering the archipelago in 1521. Spain, the colonial overlord until the end of the eighteenth century, developed plantations and factories there that produced a cigar that rivaled the havana. Indeed, the cigars were paid a similar homage and became known as *manillas.* Today, the story is somewhat different, and most cigar lovers find little that is laudable in most of the Philippine production. The reason for this is the pungent and acrid qualities of Philippine tobacco. Moreover, the tobacco, harvested mainly on the islands of Luzon and Mindanao, is reputed to lack the aromatic qualities that make for a satisfying cigar. Consequently, the filler and binder are often cut with more full-bodied tobaccos, which come largely from South America, principally from Brazil. The wrappers are also imported, mainly from Sumatra. Among the best-known brands on the market figures Flor de Isabella. Its reputation stems for the most part from the stupefying elephant's hoof: a model shaped with a large rectangular butt that leaves on the smoker's face an impression resembling the footprint of a pachyderm.

Calixto López

Calixto López, perhaps together with the brand Alhambra, is by far one of the best brands that currently are available from the Philippines. It is also one of the oldest in existence. Calixto López has been manufactured on the island of Luzon since 1881. The line offers a dozen or so models to choose from, for the most part on the mild side. The largest format in the line is represented by the Gigantes, a gargantuan indeed, measuring 8 1/2 inches in length and 3/4 inches in diameter. The Nobles, which is also 3/4 inches in diameter, is however a "mere" 6 1/2 inches long. Just as impressive are the Czar (8 inches x 3/4 inches), the Palma (7 1/4 inches x 1/2 inches), the Lonsdales (6 3/4 inches x 5/8 inches) and the Calixto López No. 1 (6 1/4 inches x 3/4 inches). Yet the smaller models are the most satisfying of the line, in particular the Corona at 5 1/2 inches in length and 4/5 inches in diameter; they are light cigars, rich in aroma yet mild in taste. The key to the survival of this brand, as for any other Philippine brand, is the low price of the cigar, one of the least expensive hand-rolled cigars available and considerably less expensive than the machine-made Cuban and Dominic models. It should be noted that Calixto López is the name of the cigar on the American market. In Europe, it is known as the Carlos V. Whether sold under Calixto López or Carlos V, the cigar is eastly distinguished by its band depicting the proud profile of the conquistador.

6 3/4 inches

Lonsdales

Known in Europe under the name Carlos V, these cigars are without a doubt the best being produced in the Philippines. This lonsdale, an intermediate format in a line that extends from the Gigantes to the Corona, is notable for its easy burning qualities and accessible price. A pleasure to smoke and somewhat peppery, it cannot be called nuanced in the effect it produces, but it nevertheless affords some pleasant surprises.

42 ring gauge

CALIXTO LÓPEZ

HECHO A MANO

SINCE 1881
A Tradition of Good Taste and Excellent Craftsmanship
PHILIPPINES

CALIXTO LÓPEZ CIGARS
25 LONSDALES SUPREMA

Zino Sumatra

Made in the Netherlands from the finest tobacco from Sumatra and Java, the Zino Drie and the Zino Jong are the best known cigars representing the so-called "Dutch flavor." The brand benefits from the powerful distribution network of the Swiss Davidoff-Oettinger group, owners of the Zino. The brand originally was produced in Honduras in 1977 as a first attempt to break into the American market. In contrast, the Zino Sumatra are intended for northern Europe, Germany in particular, where the preference is decidedly in favor of the "Dutch flavor" over the *puros* of South America favored by southern Europeans. The Zino Relax Sumatra and the Zino Classic Sumatra are part of a lighter line of cigar called the Light Line aimed at the occasional smoker and the novice. These cigars harmoniously blend the qualities of both Brazilian and Sumatran tobaccos. The same goes for the Zino Panatellas Sumatra and the Zino Cigarillos Sumatra, which are intended for the cigarillo smoker rather than for the genuine cigar lover.

Classic Sumatra

This small format is best suited to those who prefer the aroma and flavor of the choicest of Indonesian tobaccos. Its mixture of subtle and light tobaccos makes it a favorite in some European countries, especially in the Netherlands. Identifiable by the individual silver packaging of the cigars, which serves to preserve their freshness and aroma, they form the base of the Light Line Zino, a line that is completed by a series of small cigars made from Brazilian tobaccos (with brown packaging).

Glossary

Aroma: the odor a cigar develops as it is smoked.

Band: a crown of richly decorated paper that encircles the head of the cigar. First used in 1850, it became an official accoutrement of the Havana in 1884. It is an important means of identifying each brand.

Binder: intermediate wrapper, made from two half leaves.

Calibrator: instrument used for rolling cigars. It is a mold of sorts made from planks of wood between which the different formats of the cigar are shaped.

Cameroon: country in West Africa and a producer of wrappers mainly for export. Africa itself has no cigar tradition.

Casa de tabaco (tobacco shed): storeroom on a plantation where the leaves are dried and where the first fermentation takes place.

Chaveta (machete-like knife): a metal blade with a semilunar shape used by the rollers to cut the tobacco leaves.

Churchill: cigar format, around 6 3/4 in. by 3/4 in. by 1/2 oz. The name comes from the English prime minister who helped to popularize it. For the experienced smoker—it takes two hours to smoke one.

Cigarillo: small cigar with a weight less than 1/10 oz., made of shredded tobacco rather than from leaves. Machine made and often without binder, it is scorned by the connoisseur but nevertheless accounts for some ninety percent of the world's cigar production.

Cigarrito: one of the smallest formats (6 3/4 in. by 1/2 in. by about 1/10 oz.). It is as easily smoked as a cigarillo, but has the genuine qualities of a cigar.

Clarissimo: a wrapper color (green), very popular in the United States (Robert Burns, King Edward, Dutch Master).

Claro: a wrapper color (light brown).

Connecticut: Connecticut has cultivated tobacco for cigar wrappers since 1820, all destined for export (Davidoff in the Dominican Republic, Macanudo in Jamaica). The plantations are located in the Connecticut valley, from Springfield to Middletown and are concentrated around Hartford. The plants come from Cuban seeds.

Conservation: a good cigar, like a good wine, can keep up to ten to fifteen years and improves with age. The serious smoker will take care to stock the cigar in a humidified room (seventy percent humidity and a temperature not exceeding 75°F). In addition, a humidifier (see below) should be used to rehumidify the cigar prior to smoking it.

Copán (valley of): an important tobacco-producing region in Honduras.

Corojo: a plant variety grown in Cuba and used as a wrapper.

Corona: cigar format the most widely known in the world today: 5 4/5 in. by 4/5 in. by 1/4 oz. The king of cigars according to Zino Davidoff. Requires an hour and a half to smoke.

Criollo: a plant variety grown in Cuba and used as a binder and in the filler.

Culebras: cigar format made of three interwoven cigars bound together by a silk ribbon. Only Partagas and H. Upmann in Cuba and Davidoff in the Dominican Republic still produce them.

Davidoff (Zino): a legendary figure in the history of the cigar (1906-1994). Known as the creator of Châteaux (1947), Davidoff (1969) and Zino of Honduras (1977). Also the author of the celebrated *The connoisseur's Book of cigars* (1967).

Demi-tasse: also called a "lady finger." It is one of the smallest formats at 4 in. by 2/5 in. by about 1/10 oz.

Double corona: a cigar format about 7 1/2 in. by 3/4 in. by 5/8 oz. in size. It is the largest format after the especial—still commonly available, unlike the especial.

Drying: operation following the harvest which involves eliminating part of the leaves' humidity and its chlorophyll by air ("air curing") or by heating.

Escogedor: color specialist employed by the manufacturer to classify the cigars according to their tints prior to packaging.

Especial: cigar format, about 9 in. by 3/4 in. by 5/8 oz. in size. Not readily available on the market due to the lack of appropriate-sized wrappers, which are difficult to grow. This giant among giants is only for the very experienced smoker and for collectors. More than three hours are required to reduce it to ash.

Fabrica de tabaco: cigar manufacturer.

Fermentation: process involving the elimination of the tobacco's natural acidity, which comes from the resin in the leaves. Fermentation occurs at temperatures in excess of 95°F by closely stocking the leaves together on special hangars in the *casas de tabaco*.

Figurado: see Torpedo.

Filler: the contents of the cigar, made generally from three varieties of tobacco: the *ligero, the seco, the volado*.

Foot: the end of the cigar that is to be lit.

Format: standard cigar category, defined in terms of length, diameter, weight and form. Not to be confused with the model (see *Vitole*).

Galera (literally "gallery"): room at the manufactures where the cigars are rolled.

Gran corona: cigar format, about 5 4/5 in. by 5/8 in. by 2/5 oz.

Guillotina (guillotine): instrument used by the roller to cut the cigar to the desired size.

Habano: Havana.

Head: the butt of the cigar. It is either round, flat or pointed.

Hecho a mano (handmade): inscription found on the boxes which guarantees the artisanal character of the cigar's manufacturing. Since 1989, the traditional Cuban brands carry the label: *Totalmente hecho a mano—*entirely handmade.

Humidor: sealed wooden cabinet equipped with a humidifier, where cigars from the humidified room in which they are kept are stored a few weeks before being smoked.

Jalapa (valley): important cigar-producing region between Honduras and Nicaragua.

Ligero: a very aromatic tobacco, obtained from the uppermost leaves of the plant which have received the most exposure from the sun.

Lighting: cut the cigar before hand with a cigar guillotine or with the fingernails or by biting the end, and light the base with a wooden match, stem of cedar or a lighter. The Cubans have the habit of dunking the end of the cigar in a cup of sugary coffee or in rum, a practice which purists find abominable. It serves no purpose to warm the cigar before lighting it or to lick it.

Lonsdale: cigar format, about 6 in. by 5/8 in. by 3/8 oz. in size. More svelte and longer than the churchill, its name comes from the English aristocrat Lord Lonsdale.

Maduro: color of a wrapper—dark brown.

Mendes, Arnaldo Tamayo: Cuban cosmonaut and the first man to smoke a cigar in outer space (on September 18, 1980).

Nicotiana: see Tobacco.

Olor dominicano: local Dominican variety of plant, yielding very light tobacco.

Panetela: cigar format about 6 in. by 1/2 in. by 1/5 oz. Its long, elegant shape is perfectly suited for the feminine smoker. A larger format, the gran panetela (7 3/8 in. by 3/5 in. by 3/8 oz.), is less available today.

Piloto cubano: a Dominican variety of plant grown from Cuban seeds and yielding very aromatic tobacco.

Plant: young plant from a seedling used for establishing a subculture. Once matured, the plant will be composed of six different tiers (for a *corojo*) from bottom to top: the *libra de pie* (the free foot), which is used as the filler and binder; the *uno y medio* (the one and a half), used as a binder; the *centro ligero* (the light middle) and the *centro fino* (the fine middle), used as wrappers; the *centro gordo* (the thick middle), for wrappers and filler; and the *corona* (the crown), used as a binder. Each tier is separately harvested at one week intervals, or forty days total to harvest each *corojo* plant.

Prominente: Cuban name for a double corona.

Puro: Spanish synonym for a cigar.

Robusto: cigar format, around 5 in. by 3/4 in. by 2/5 oz. Very fashionable at the moment, it develops the strength of a churchill in a fairly short time (forty minutes). For the experienced smoker.

Roller: see Torcedor.

San Andres (valley): main tobacco-producing region for cigars in Mexico. Located in the state of Veracruz.

San Vincente: Dominican variety of plant, from Cuban seeds. The name derives from a plantation in the Vuelta Abajo from where the seeds originated.

Seco: a tobacco less rich than the *ligero*, but of a more subtle aroma, obtained from leaves from the middle of the plant.

Small corona: cigar format (approximately 5 in. by 3/5 in. by 1/4 oz.), the most common format after the corona.

Sumatra: island belonging to Indonesia and the country's principal producer of cigar tobacco, along with Java and Borneo. Known for producing excellent wrappers.

Tabacos: name given by the Tainos Indians to the dry rolled leaves they used to smoke. By accident, the name would be attributed to the plant itself, which the Tainos called *cohiba*.

Tabaquero: laborer in the cigar factories, or anyone involved in the manufacturing process.

Tapados: long blankets of white cotton suspended by pickets to protect the plants grown for wrappers from the sun, the wind and parasites.

Taste: sensation left in the mouth after smoke from the cigar comes into contact with saliva. More or less heavy depending on whether the cigar is full-bodied or light. According to the natural acidity of the tobacco, the cigar is also more or less acrid, sweet or sugary.

Tobacco: aromatic plant from the *Solanaceae* family. When dried, its leaves are used as smoking tobacco. The genus *Nicotiana* includes sixty different species, grouped in three subgenera: *Nicotiana tabacum*, *Nicotiana rustica* and *Nicotiana petunioides* (the latter is grown only for ornamental purposes). *Nicotiana rustica* is the tobacco plant smoked by the Indians at the time the Europeans arrived. It is still grown in Eastern Europe (the Ukraine, Poland) and in North Africa and Pakistan. It yields mediocre tobacco and is mainly used to make snuff. Originally from Mexico, *Nicotiana tabacum* is the most widely used species today because of its strong aromatic qualities. For cigar tobacco, it has been used to breed some remarkable hybrids: *havanensis* in Cuba, *brasiliensis* in South America, *virginica* in North America and *purpurea* in Asia.

Torcedor (literally, "twister"): roller. Laborer in the factories who is assigned the task of rolling the cigars by hand.

Torpedo: cigar format shaped like a torpedo, called "piramides" when the head is pointed, and "bombshell" when both ends are pointed.

Très petit corona: cigar format, about 4 in. by 5/8 in. by 1/5 oz.

Vega: tobacco plantation; more specifically, the collection of fields making up a plantation.

Veguero: plantation laborer.

Vista (view): colorful ornamentation often found on the inside cover of the cigar box.

Vitola: model produced by a brand which, besides its well-defined formal characteristics (see Format), is also christened with a commercial name.

Vitophilia: the collecting of cigar bands and vistas.

Volado: weakly aromatic tobacco but with excellent burning qualities, obtained from the leaves on the lowest tier of the plant, those least exposed to the sun.

Vuelta Abajo: region in the province of Pinar del Rio, located in the western part of the island of Cuba. The foremost tobacco-growing land in the world. Some 99,000 acres of land are reserved solely for the cultivation of tobacco. It includes some of the most famous vegas, such as San Luis and San Jose y Martinez. The other tobacco-growing regions of Cuba are Partidos, Semi Vuelta, Remedio and Oriente (these last three regions produce tobacco for domestic consumption only.)

Wrapper: exterior leaf in which the tobacco is wrapped. It is made from half a tobacco leaf.

Yaqui (valley): the second most important tobacco-producing region in the world. Located in the northwest of the Dominican Republic.

Photo credits

All photographs in the book are by Fanny Bruno, apart from those listed below :

Davidoff & Cie, Genève : p. 72, p. 73, p. 74 (top), p. 75 (all), p. 84, p. 85, p. 114;
J.-L. Charmet : p. 100, p. 126 (bottom left), p. 132 (bottom left), p. 136;
Explorer : p. 102, p. 103 J.-P. Courau; p. 133 J. Darche; p. 119 M. Evans;
p. 122 (top) M. Koene; p. 126 (top) G. Martin;
Gamma : p. 10 (top, bottom x 2), p. 11 M. Deville; p. 10 (middle) A. Duclos;
p. 8 (top), p. 12 (top), p. 13 (bottom) Ferry; p. 12 (bottom) G. Kremer; p. 13 (top) R. Wollman;
musée de la Marine, Paris : p. 8 (bottom), p. 70, p. 118 (bottom), p. 122 (bottom);
Padron : p. 123 (bottom); Matthieu Prier : p. 66 (bottom), back cover;
Roger Viollet : p. 14, p. 126 (middle), p. 137; Te-Amo p. 127 (bottom right).

Designed and produced by Copyright, Paris
Art directors: Ute-Charlotte Hettler, Hervé Tardy and Jacqueline Leymarie
Illustrations: Lara Gass

The photographs of the cigars were taken at *La Casa Del Habano*
- 1434 Sherbrooke O - Montreal, Quebec

English adaptation edited by John Herrick, David Stevens and Elizabeth Ayre

Anne-Marie Chéné would like to thank Raffi Kotchounian of Vasco Cigars for his help in the selection of cigars,
Vince Guzzo for his precious Havanas, Daniel Rioux for his generosity and judicious comments,
and Michel Dupont for his patience and understanding.

Copyright thanks all of the brands which assisted in assembling the necessary information and documents.
We also thank Lew Rothman of J.R. Tobacco Company, 11 East 45th Street, New York,
and Frank Pinto of Barclay-Rex, 7 Maiden Lane, New York, and especially Esther Rohrer of Davidoff, Geneva,
and Olivier Fau of La Licorne, 5, place Rouaix, Toulouse, who lent us his precious collection of rings and labels.